Benyamini's text zooms in on the signifier "Israeli" in a stunning philosophic-psychoanalytic hermeneutic of self-analysis. It unpacks a kaleidoscopic heterogeneity, produced by phantasmatic dreams of past and future projected upon a present endlessly circling the unrepresented Real of trauma. The text embodies and tells of a pulsating vitality, that seeks both home and structure. Conflicted elements of this vitality continuously re-inscribe a precarious balance of complementarity and negation. In this complex, intricate ambiguity Benyamini portrays the dangers and appeals of the unequivocal, fragmenting figure of Netanyahu, before and after October 7th. The book offers a remarkable explanation of the disquieting and gripping fascination with Israel.

Shlomit Yadlin-Gadot, *PhD, Chair of the Psychotherapy Program, School of Medicine, Tel-Aviv University. Co-author of "Lacanian Psychoanalysis: A Contemporary Introduction" (Routledge 2023)*

A Psycho-Political Analysis of Netanyahu's Israel: The Israeli Anxiety brings continental philosophy, psychoanalysis, biblical studies, and political theory to bear on the most intimate and deep-seated features of contemporary Israel. By weaving together these diverse fields of knowledge, it offers a fresh and penetrating critique of Israeli society, culture, and politics—from its origins to its current crises. This is a bold and original work by one of the most creative Israeli thinkers of our time.

Yotam Hotam, *PhD, University of Haifa. Author of: "Critiques of Theology: German-Jewish Intellectuals and the Religious Sources of Secular Thought" (SUNY 2023)*

I0094020

A Psycho-Political Analysis of Netanyahu's Israel

This book weaves together philosophical, theological, psychoanalytical, and political paradigms, providing both a historicization and a theorization of the Israeli experience and encompassing social-political events in recent history and life in Israel.

Born out of Itzhak Benyamini's subjective experience as an "Israeli," a "Mizrahi" (a Hebrew term referring to a Jewish person whose origin derives from the Muslim world), and a "civilian," this book provides an in-depth discussion of the psychical and philosophical ramifications of recent sociopolitical events in Israel. Throughout chapters discussing topics such as identity, the uncanny, and the political ontology of time, Benyamini sheds light on the uncanny feelings of Israelis following Benyamin Netanyahu's long term in office. The book deciphers the multilayered Israeli anxiety and exposes the measure of complexity that such a psycho-political identity accumulates.

A multidisciplinary work combining sociological, psychoanalytical, and philosophical thought, this book will be of interest to scholars, students, and professionals in these fields and those who would like to learn more about Israeli culture.

Itzhak Benyamini teaches at the Bezalel Academy of Art and Design in Jerusalem and in the Psychotherapy Program at Tel Aviv University. Dr. Benyamini is the author of numerous books and articles, which have been translated into English, French, and German. His main interests cover, as well as weave together, the intricate relations between psychoanalytic theory and religious and political discourses.

Philosophy and Psychoanalysis
Jon Mills
Series Editor

Philosophy and Psychoanalysis is dedicated to current developments and cutting-edge research in the philosophical sciences, phenomenology, hermeneutics, existentialism, logic, semiotics, cultural studies, social criticism, and the humanities that engage and enrich psychoanalytic thought through philosophical rigor. With the philosophical turn in psychoanalysis comes a new era of theoretical research that revisits past paradigms while invigorating new approaches to theoretical, historical, contemporary, and applied psychoanalysis. No subject or discipline is immune from psychoanalytic reflection within a philosophical context including psychology, sociology, anthropology, politics, the arts, religion, science, culture, physics, and the nature of morality. Philosophical approaches to psychoanalysis may stimulate new areas of knowledge that have conceptual and applied value beyond the consulting room reflective of greater society at large. In the spirit of pluralism, *Philosophy and Psychoanalysis* is open to any theoretical school in philosophy and psychoanalysis that offers novel, scholarly, and important insights in the way we come to understand our world.

Titles in this series:

R. D. Laing in the Twenty-First Century: Sanity, Therapy, Love
Michael Guy Thompson, Fritjof Capra and Douglas Kirsner

Monstrosity and the Psychoanalytic Dimensions of the Uncanny
Rodrigo Gonsalves

Selected Essays of Ladson Hinton: Psychoanalytic and Existential Reflections on Shame and Temporality
Hessel Willemsen

A Psycho-Political Analysis of Netanyahu's Israel: The Israeli Anxiety
Itzhak Benyamini

A Psycho-Political Analysis of Netanyahu's Israel

The Israeli Anxiety

Itzhak Benyamini

Translated by Marianna Barr

Routledge
Taylor & Francis Group
LONDON AND NEW YORK

Designed cover image: "© Demonstration near the house of Netanyahu, Jerusalem, 1 of August 2020", by Itzhak Benyamini

First published 2026
by Routledge
4 Park Square, Milton Park, Abingdon, Oxon OX14 4RN

and by Routledge
605 Third Avenue, New York, NY 10158

Routledge is an imprint of the Taylor & Francis Group, an informa business

Translated by Marianna Barr

For Product Safety Concerns and Information please contact our EU representative GPSR@taylorandfrancis.com. Taylor & Francis Verlag GmbH, Kaufingerstraße 24, 80331 München, Germany.

Trademark notice: Product or corporate names may be trademarks or registered trademarks, and are used only for identification and explanation without intent to infringe.

British Library Cataloguing-in-Publication Data
A catalogue record for this book is available from the British Library

ISBN: 978-1-041-12945-5 (hbk)
ISBN: 978-1-041-12943-1 (pbk)
ISBN: 978-1-003-66733-9 (ebk)

DOI: 10.4324/9781003667339

Typeset in Times New Roman
by SPi Technologies India Pvt Ltd (Straive)

Contents

Acknowledgments

I am deeply indebted to Marianna Barr, who has translated this book with such skill and lingual sensitivity, thereby adding a quality dimension to the depiction of the Israeli experience and perhaps to the choice of my Hebrew words as well, both of which border on the untranslatable to non-Israeli readers. I wish to thank Dr. Jon Mills, editor of the series "Philosophy and Psychoanalysis" at Routledge, for his interest in the book and his readiness to promote a space of philosophical and psychoanalytical thought during such challenging, charged times. To the editing board of Routledge, Katie Randal, Prisha Revar, Manon Berset and Divya Muthu, I am deeply grateful for their prompt and professional treatment of this text, making it such an informative, pleasurable experience. Lastly, my gratitude goes to Avishay Rubin for his extended help in preparing the text for submission. On a more personal level, I wish to thank Dr. Raphael Zagury-Orly, my close friend and colleague, whose depth of thought and political commitment have been for me a philosophical as well as a moral compass, with the deeper level of his inspiration being the inevitable relation between the two. Finally, I thank my loved one, my partner, Dr. Orit Yushinsky, who shares my life and my thoughts, and in her wisdom, always points to the ethical dimension that the word must consider in its encounter with life and the world.

The Feeling of Benyamini: Foreword by the Translator, Marianna Barr

Theoreticians, scholars, and authors have at times referred to the act/process/ outcome of translation in very violent and even traumatic terms. "To translate is to violate," asserted Ruth Nevo in her "Bialik: caught in a world whose God is dead" (*Israel Poetry International Web*); in his comprehensive study of language and translation, *After Babel* (3rd ed. [1998]), George Steiner argues that "like breathing, it [translation] is subject to obstruction and homicidal breakdown." Some of the 20 theses that foreword Emily Apter's monograph *The Translation Zone* (2006), which discusses the more political aspects/implications of translation, are also worth mentioning: "The translation zone is a war zone; translation is an Oedipal assault on the mother tongue; translation is a traumatic loss of the native tongue; translation is the language of planets and monsters." Personally, I remain partial to Paul Ricoeur's *Sur la traduction* (2004 [*On Translation* 2007]) in which he examines translation as a relation to otherness: when we accept the indispensability of otherness, then both the original language as well as the target one benefit from it. For Ricoeur, as for Steiner, navigating through our world requires continual translation, and so Ricoeur envisages translation as a process of mourning rather than one of melancholy. There is loss, no doubt, but there is also invaluable gain. The working-through itself. Which brings us to Itzhak Benyamini.

I had the privilege, as well as the indescribable challenge – which I shall nevertheless attempt to describe – to transpose Benyamini's writings from the Hebrew language as foreign to itself into English that is foreign both to the Hebrew as well as to itself, in Benyamini's terms. Benyamini's writing – to which he himself refers as an independent entity impinging on his being – may be characterized as a psycho-philosophical-political-poetical, imaging *play* (at times quite humorous). In his abstruse style, Benyamini, on the one hand, shows us how hard and at times hopeless the attempt is to decipher the Israeli being in all its aspects. On the other hand, once we have started striding on this terrain – and the act of translation forces us to do so – and the snow has melted, bluebells fill the grounds. Benyamini dreams of an Israeli society no longer lacerated by the existing ethnic, religious, and political polarities; a society at peace with itself as well as with its others. This could come to pass only when every one of us recognizes and follows her/his desire, as according to Lacan, in whose writings Benyamini is erudite, only when we do not follow this path, are we *truly* guilty. Hence, the anxiety. But Benyamini is painfully aware of the fact that he is dreaming. He meanders in his dream world, employing a vast repository of signifiers, both in style and in content.

Indeed, beyond the apparent affinity to Freud and Lacan, as well as his wide philosophical cognizance, Benyamini borrows from mathematical and physical concepts, which transcend into images that can only be *experienced*, not read, nor written, nor conceptualized – but felt. There is no pure or simple and certainly not categorical or stable political, psychoanalytical, or philosophical stance. All is open-ended, including the very writing itself: "The act of writing depends neither on the author nor on one concept or another nor on the readers but is suspended in the air without any support like an acrobat suspended in the air without a rope under him…" Benyamini tells us. He lifts the mirror up to us – moving it vertically, horizontally, and sidewise. He shows us, much like philosophy and psychoanalysis, that our journey is endless and open-ended. As readers, we do not have the right to put an end to it or to close it, and neither does the author. In Benyamini's "fantasy," as he terms it, all authors, translators, and readers alike may do is attempt to describe the journey and point to the impediments and obstructions along the way. Benyamini converses with Walter Benjamin's "The task of the Translator," particularly regarding the concept of the "nucleus" of all languages. But contrary to Benjamin, who imagines the original language as the forest and the target one as being exterior to it,[1] Benyamini's texts invited me into the *thicket* of the forest and insisted that I remain there, as for Benyamini everything begins and ends in the thicket; he brings the image, letter, and word to his texts both as iconic as well as transcendent to themselves. Benyamini's style does not respect grammatical rules nor constraining paradigms – such as the academic one – but is in a constant flow and flux of metonyms, antonyms, homophones, and homonyms. When they are not available, he makes them up. Furthermore, Benyamini makes extensive use of Hebrew roots. In Hebrew, many dissimilar and at times even opposed terms are branched out from a common root. This characteristic ties in with Benyamini's experience as a writer: everything contains its opposite and vice versa. All of this richness is, of course, lost in translation, which warrants melancholy. But what is the process, the "working-through" that has led me to mourning, which in our context is the gain?

If we must confine Benyamini's writing to one term – which we do not have to do – then the nearest one would be poetry. In the same sense that Derrida is a poet. For what is the resistance to rules, authoritativeness, and decisiveness if not poetry? Not to mention neologisms. As a rule, in poetry, we are hooked first and foremost by the prosody. It is the prosody that draws us to delve into the depths of the content and the imagery. But as successful as we might be in deciphering those, the poem might remain unresolved and continue to haunt us. Such was my experience with Benyamini's texts: I was allured as a close but confused reader, further confused and rendered innocent. To be able to feel Benyamini's writing, I had to become an innocent reader who is prepared to be confused. Innocent does not mean ignorant, for neither the mind nor the psyche can be entirely unburdened, but unbiased under a temporary willing suspension of knowledge. We have to deconstruct our knowledge in order to recreate our innocence, even if it can only be to a certain degree. And in the process, conflicting feelings surface. For me, translating Benyamini's texts has been an intense process of taking my clothes off, putting them back on, altering their hems, their width, their length, seeing through them, and continually wondering whether they fit me or not, but mostly fearing damage or tearing them. I have been given an exemplary demonstration of how language cannot represent itself. It can only try. Paradoxically speaking, it is precisely this flexibility and this insubordination to rules and conventions of writing that endows the text with its singularity, which I had to be so careful not to ruin. Not to explicate what the author had no wish to clarify.

Benyamini does not spare himself doubt nor criticism, a feeling that has permeated me throughout my work and driven me to be more and more reflective in and of his texts. In his attempt, for example, to struggle with his neologism, the "psycho-political," Benyamini asserts: "As rationalistic and as intelligible as the term psycho-political may seem, it is an onerous obnubilation of its conflictual terms, the psychical and the political." Who am I to argue? But my heart goes out to him; *I feel* his struggle. So, I struggled with what might be the best way to bring this feeling to the English reader; in this struggle, I discovered both aptitude, which brought about enormous pride and joy, as well as failure, which, when it occurred, filled me up with exasperation. But Benyamini himself would rather remain in the metonymic world than clarify the situation for us for in his "Elementary Preface":

> [...] language could be an opportunity for us to find ourselves through the reading, like the lake in which the waters of the territorial language are flushed in intimacy from the reader's mouth back to his/her eye without any possibility to get to know the interior stream of the lingual waters in the lake of language. (here, p. xxii)

For Benyamini, when the intention is to write off the obnubilation of a concept, that is when the concept collapses. Rather than psychoanalyzing the occurrences and the figures he discusses, or philosophizing on them, he illustrates their complexity in the wordiness itself. Because the reality of his themes is so complex and absurd, so must be the writing about it. In this sense, the writing is an icon of its content. Therefore, I had to let Benyamini confuse me and learn how to pass on this confusion to the foreign reader; in other words, discard the fear of being considered an incompetent translator for the task. In that, I have learned how to truly respect another. It is also what I recommend for the reader, both the Hebrew as well as the foreign one.

Note

1 "Unlike a work of literature, translation does not find itself in the center of the language forest but on the outside facing the wooded ridge; it calls into it without entering, aiming at that single spot where the echo is able to give, in its own language, the reverberation of the work in the alien one". Walter Benjamin, "The Task of the Translator.", in *Selected Writings – Vol. 1*, M. Bullock and M.W. Jennings, eds., Cambridge, Mass & London: The Belknap Press of Harvard University Press, 1992, pp. 258–259.

Elementary Preface to the Isra-External Edition of "A Psycho-Political Analysis of Netanyahu's Israel: The Israeli Anxiety"

Author's abstract

The present preface is composing itself in an attempt to provide itself and us with an answer regarding its identity, and it addresses me for this purpose, and I am writing it for its own purposes. This was preceded by the imposition I had imposed on it to compose itself as a preface to be translated into foreign languages and constitute an aperture for the non-Israeli readers of the book on the Israeli anxiety. Out of the apparent author within me, namely the apparent sense of an author holding masterful intentions that the written word is presumed to satisfy and assign meaning for him, this preface sets out to examine its status, as well as its gender,[2] given my proprietary demands as its author who fences it in with its tarrying masculinity. Consequently, the preface yields its meaning as psycho-political and underscores the relation between the author and his word, between the psychical and the political, and between the preface itself and the book. As the preface has written itself through me writing it, it has developed a phantasmatic theory, both in the sense that it is a theory bearing a phantasmatic weight and in the sense that it examines the phantasmatic space of the translation's interpretation as ingrained in the psychical struggling with its hallucinatory dynamic within the space of languages. For this purpose, the preface takes advantage of my editorial experience regarding the translations of Sigmund Freud's meta-psychological essays from his German into our Hebrew. We seek out the Hebrew in the German and translate the Hebrew which the German (imagined by us) imagines into Hebrew: a translation from Hebrew into Hebrew.

1   The words of the present preface (introducing itself to itself as well) originate from a nucleolar **thing** ["Davar" in Hebrew], which they extract from the chapters before us and which they aim to serve. "Thing" in Hebrew is a double entendre: as *das Ding*, which belongs to the realm of the substance – the bone, the *ousia* ("Etzem" in Hebrew)[3], dating back to the Akkadian *eşemtu as* bodily mold (from which derive the bones of the body, the physical contour, the essence of the thing, individuality, and substance), as well as a thing [Davar] in the realms of *logos* ["Dibra" in Hebrew] and *parole* (speech and word) ["Dibur" in Hebrew]. Such is the double entendre of a single

Hebrew word, *which designates two words in Hebrew*, identical in sound, writing, and vocalization. This duality is emphasized to understand the affective realness and the philology of the nucleus that it too speaks on behalf of the present treatise. This wordiness will orient us toward a clarification regarding language in general (and from this to clarification regarding identity as a whole, including Israeli identity), whose rudiments are foreign languages, including the ones not yet acknowledged by the lingual chronological history, and are exposed in the act of translation when the foreign word encounters its selfhood and becomes one with it. This wordiness will also orient us toward the logic of the present preface itself.

If there is such a thing as a language of truth, a tensionless and even silent depository of the ultimate secrets for which all thought strives, then this language of truth is - the true language. And this very language, in whose divination and description lies the only perfection for which a philosopher can hope, is concealed in concentrated fashion in translations.
(Walter Benjamin, "The Task of the Translator")[1]

2   The very logos drives the preface to speak its being individual and nucleolar to itself, insofar as the thing is struggling to explain itself or warrant its existence as a preface that does not elucidate what will follow but introduces its being the "pre" of the thing. The author's hope is for his deviousness to obscure the convergence of the thing into itself, and that precisely in this convergence, the thing will touch upon the urgent questions of the (Israeli) psycho-political.

The nucleolar word "thing" considers the book's non-Israeli readers as its addressees. Still, the math is one of subtraction and not one of addition because it subtracts the Israeli subtrahends from the global ones and then imagines the products of the difference as addressees. However, they are becoming the conceptual addressees of the word "thing" and not necessarily its actual addressees. Them being an addressee is the very conceptuality in which they dwell, as if the word "thing" addresses those already here as the conceptuality of "non-Israelis." The presence of this conceptuality will be the key to what follows in which the preface will speak of its precedence and its conceptual objective, the address for which it makes time.

Since the present preface conceptualizes its selfhood to exhaustion, it could be a comic gesture to the comicality of the dialectic of Hegel's *Preface to the Phenomenology of Spirit*, both of which envelop themselves in a countenance of solemn science.

3   The elementary preface moves *alongside* its pretentious-non-materializing objective; it is self-frustrating to not achieve the desired goal and therefore directs itself to a lateral move to begin with. So, the pretention of the preface is a priori lateral to itself because the very pretention to preface is to represent the content of the book. In effect, this pretention is made lateral

because the present preface evades the pretentious laterality toward an objective in itself (as addressing a particular kind of readers). Namely, if there is already laterality brought about by the dimension that cannot be materialized, then the preface lateralizes itself far from the pretention itself toward narcissistic parasitism on its very being as lateral.

In these self-multiplying lateralities, in this performative theater of lateral lateralities, there is a possibility to obtain more accessible access to the chapters of this book, which are also attempts to look sideways in the sense of not siding with any particular political stance. Looking sideways from laterality or from unilaterality, which is not really possible and perhaps merely a reference imagined for the non-Israeli readers, may enable such a lateral viewpoint without choosing a side in the perilous psycho-political.

Therefore, the pretention aims to explain the scheme of things in the present book to non-Israelis, but from a sideways shift that accumulates the non-Israelis *into the post-factum* written to be also the **pre** for the Israelis as already formulated in the chapters, for which the word rewrites itself here from within the logic of the preface.

This will be an accumulation that treasures for itself the way the German language understands the Hebrew embodied in the German word. The German prefix "vor" as being both a temporal **pre** as well as a synchronous physical **contiguous** makes literal the status of the non-Israeli readers as ones that may be geographically lateral to Israel but precedes Israel ontologically, in a manner that makes it possible for Israelis to understand their interior Israeliness for themselves, and **themselves alone**. As a formula, "for themselves alone" may be formulated for them from an external viewpoint, even though it may be *for them as Israelis, like the exterior*, or that of those that are exterior *to them*, such as the Germans, the Ethiopians, or the Greeks. And, if this is their **external** viewpoint, then it is the result of the self-examination that sets them apart. "Themselves alone" may be inscribed via a distinction between their being and their non-being (this expression generates a sharp distinction between "them" and others or between what is "theirs" and what belongs to others or between their essence as "they" themselves and the essence of the others as "they" themselves).

4   The apparent intention is to provide a complementary historical and cultural background to the contentions that appear in the chapters. However, all this is inscribed in Hebrew (not only with the aid of Hebrew but also literally **through it** in its being of beings and exchanging Hebrew as being for its being *written* Hebrew), which stems from that feeling of intimacy that the word shares with its readers in Hebrew.

This preface is to be found within the tension between the apparent intention of the word as directed to the exterior and its interior tendency to speak to its internal readers and traverse them **interiorly**. The background it provides is meant for the in-between readers: those suspended in the air between those imagined and those pictured here. In this sense, the in-between readers yield a **logical** axis regarding the relations between the Israeli and the non-Israeli in its encounter with the depth of the Israeli anxiety in its innermost intimacy both to itself and exteriorly. This intimacy cannot escape being exterior because it is inscribed herewith under the words themselves.

Hence, both the conceptual expressions presented in this preface and the scheme of the opening copy their significance for the reader by virtue of their concrete performance in the act of writing.

5　**An almost lateral** clarification regarding the phantasmatic theory on the *dwelling of a foreign language* – such as Hebrew – *within an original language* – such as German, similarly to a baby virus that *incubates* until the moment the translation disease *breaks out* in the body carrying it (not necessarily as a foreign substance but as compatible with the very biological mechanism that even duplicates it). Perhaps, this is a revelatory perception in the sense Walter Benjamin discusses it, but *not* in the sense that he refers to the origin of truth as a *thing*.

Moreover, *the foreign language* tells us that it is an expression of another non-accessible or exterior language into which Hebrew is translated. On the other hand, *the original language* tells us that it is "our" language being translated, while the "our" may be displaced to any subject anywhere. For example, here, Hebrew may be perceived as the foreign language, while German may have the status of the original language from which we translate.

But is there not here a slight mix-up? The foreign language is foreign in relation to the original language when we translate from German into Hebrew, and is alien to the German. In contrast, the *original language* is in its self-perception the original when translated from; but for us, the original may be precisely the target language, for it is our origin. It, therefore, seems that both the *original* and the *target language* have slightly deceived us in their definitions, and that it all depends on the direction of the translation and where we stand or that we are always aiming at the direction of the original language, which is ours but foreign to the language of the translated text. Namely, *we translate into* an *original language which we extract from the original language to which our language is foreign, which is to say that we extract from the Hebrew-as-foreign language within the translated-as-original text for our Hebrew source.* How confusing.

This linguistic confusion may either be resolved or die at the hands of the following passages about the phantasmatic theory of translation:

In language **A** incubate units of foreign language **B**, which are revealed to the world in translation and are embodied as the act of translation from the original to the foreign. The translation is the materialization of the interior potential of the foreign within the original; it is what drives the original to its beloved destination in the foreign language at the end of a long exile. The translation machine is a moving truck, as we see written on many trucks in Greece: *metaphor*, which in ancient Greek means "*meta –* forward," "*phorein –* move," and in modern terms denotes transportation, moving, or transference.

Perhaps, the word "thing" echoes the thingness of language in Walter Benjamin, a romantic or mystic of the *original* that in his "Task of the Translator" pins us in the metaphysics of yearning for the *Thing* (das Ding) as the nucleus of languages. His chapter echoes the idea that translation, in its significant task, encounters the *Thing* at which the translated word is aiming during the efforts exerted in the labor of translation. In this way, the translator touches upon the general language of truth, the truth of the thing, even more so than the author of the original text and the original language.

But in our peculiar idea, the metaphysical premise is not the Benjamin's connection within the original word *between the thing and the intention for the thing (phenomenological intentionality)*. We are speaking of the fragments of the signified within the word, endless fragments of signified, whose "origins" exist in *synchronicity* with many of the target languages, not in the sense that the original language actually dwells only in the truth of the foreign one, but insofar as we experience the language of the translated text mentally as holding our language hostage as an interior foreign language to itself before becoming a target language. Or is it that the present fantasy stems from the Benyaminian fantasy or both that of Walter's and Itzhak's?

Let us clarify. The German word hides entities expressed solely in translation, entities such as the Hebrew. This is not a chronological perception of language because German does not really know Hebrew, but how the German exists means that retrospectively the Hebrew lies there in the original German, and in reverse, and precisely for this reason, *not* retrospectively as well (because of the non-theoretical purposefulness of the translation task, which struggles with the *here and now*). Thus, in the German word lie linguistic perspectives of Hebrew, Arabic, Latin, and others for the very same word.

For example, the German word "Lust" contains idiosyncratic Hebrew essentialities of the words delight, pleasure, lustfulness, and jouissance. This is the meaning of a "**semantic field**." This field does not contain the signifiers of the original word; however, only for me, as a Hebrew speaker, it includes signifiers from my language, which is foreign to German. In the act of translation, all those Hebrew words incubated in the swamp of the German word "Lust" hatch, and the word "pleasure" that was trapped in the German original word finds itself and becomes one with itself. Choosing the word "pleasure" over the other ones in the same semantic field, in which the German word "Lust" is both held and holding, is the result of our assumption that this Hebrew word is the most compatible with the German one, by our understanding of the word in our *Hebraic* *being*. This is also true according to the convention that a good translation is done by a translator whose native tongue is the target one.

Thus, *the translation is not from German into Hebrew but rather from Hebrew through German back into Hebrew*. The translation is from **pleasure** as a word in German to **pleasure** as a word in Hebrew. The moving truck has transported the word "pleasure" from Germany to Israel. This is perhaps the redemption of the word.

This metaphysical issue has implications for our present discussion of Israeliness and its non-Israeliness nucleus and, further on, for our concept of the psycho-political. This does not imply that the origins of the political are psychical or the opposite, nor that there is a translation here, but rather a sneaky transition from the thing to the thing itself, from the political to the political, from the psychical to the psychical, from the non-Israeli to the non-Israeli, and from the Israeli to the Israeli. The translation is not from one essence to another but from foundation **A** within **B** to **A** accumulated in **B**.

Namely, translation is a non-actuality that acts in the world as a means of exchange or passageway from one thing to another (and not from Benyamin's thing to other signifiers). Translation does not exist in reality but is merely an act of the thing that remains in its becoming **another itself** and is revealed to itself in its nuclearism. In this sense, this is a tautology insofar as tautology as a concept may contain the meaning of the dynamic in which the one becomes itself and is revealed to its fuller self.

Perhaps, we are nevertheless Walter Benjamins... Perhaps behind the succession of verbalizations of the same thing in various languages, we are still trapped in the fantasy of the one thing. Perhaps.

But let us not leave the perhaps in its perhapsness. Let us describe the following dynamic of delusion: For Benjamin, the word **a** in the translated text refers to thing #, and the translation of the word in the translating text is **א**, which in the act of translation responds to the language of things – *Die Sprache der Dinge* – in the encounter with the *das Ding* or with the object #.

The phantasmatic theory here does not suggest an encounter with the things or with the thing # but rather a meeting of the translating language with its own words, such as **א** within the translated language **within** the word **a**. Both the translating language and the target language are being displaced; in the act of translating or moving by the metaphoric **truck a**, the word **a** as *German substance* is displaced to a word that is also **א** as *Hebrew substance*.

Perhaps, Benjamin's position is an item in this theoretical delusion, that when the anchor for this delusion of the translator's task is that he moves **א** to **א** via **a** while having illusions about #'s existence. The present analysis of Benjamin's perception is a part and parcel of this complete delusion as well.

Perhaps, "Benjamin" here functions as # for the present phantasmatic theory, which the preface sustains for itself.

6   This collection comprises eight chapters defined as *psycho-political*, a definition under which they are intended for the ISRA-external readers. The ISRA-external as a term is a tri-dimensional topological broadening or deepening of the bi-dimensional arithmetic subtraction mentioned above of the non-Israelis.

The act of writing here is hovering in the zone between the bi- and the tri-dimensional in an attempt to understand what grips the *trans-Israeli* that exists between its negation and its being exterior and distinct. What is between subtracting and exteriorizing the essence, and **what** exists outside the Israeli existence?

The act of writing is contingent neither on the author nor on one concept or another, nor on the readers, but is suspended in the air without any support, like an acrobat suspended in the air without a rope under him over the immeasurable void between the bi- and the tri-dimensional. Perhaps, the suspension in this peculiar air seems hallucinatory to us, for we wonder about the ropeless suspension. However, if we fathomed that another illusion is covering this fantasy, it would no longer be perceived as a fantasy. Such is the author's delusion, not in respect of his intentions but in respect of his being, for there is something of the intentions and nothing of the author. Intentions and no author, so whose are the intentions? It seems that dependence on suspension in the air also touches upon who or what the writer is. Yuval Barel[4] reminded me of the story he had told me some time ago. One of his students argued that Hebrew was born from German, and this plot dwelled in a conscience unaware of its memory. That student writes his story through my friend and me, but in formative crystallization, he both exists and does not exist. The plot is both present and absent. We are in the bi-dimensional of the linear story but not yet in the tri-dimensional of the spatial formalization, regarding the comprehensive question of translation. The student also spoke of the birth of Hebrew in German. So, the formalization has become the constant habitat of Hebrew in German. Namely, some intentions or opinions made their way like a parasite via several authors until they reached their destination, perhaps like the DNA that multiplies through living organisms.

We have found that the act of translation is situated in two-and-a-half dimensions: between the bi-dimensionality of the imaginary-visual linearity and the tri-dimensional spatiality, in the form of a half that is not quite perceivable. But what is that "half" if not the traversal of the space between the two and the tri and the collapse of both into another non-existent dimension created by the writing, a non-visual universe created by the most unconventional means – letters and words. As visual as they may be, they symbolize non-visual concepts.

The words gaze at themselves and narrate themselves in homage to Merav Shalom-Zehavi,[5] whose poetry of letters pressures and rescues words from their bi-dimensionality on the page, traversing toward the independent tri-. Her poetic constitution is psycho-political because the exteriorization processes each letter to its psychical political. In its inscription *a la* Joyce's *Finnegans Wake*, English expands to an additional dimension, from the horizontal to the vertical. Still, it fails, and the reader turns at once from the page outside and back to himself on the page. But poetry leaves the reader halfway between the bi and the tri. Such is also the act of writing, generally speaking, which is not really on the page of the bi, nor is it on the tri of our global, physical state of affairs as living creatures. The psycho-political as a concept is writing itself between the political and the psychic, as if between a particular dimension and a higher one, when it is unclear which is where and perhaps they switch places – at times, the psychical is up and the political is down, and vice versa.

The following chapters engender a tri-dimensional relation between them, which calls for a topological broadening and strengthening of the present discourse through the notion of the psycho-political and a diagnosis of the relationship between them (as in Jacques Lacan's concept of the Name-of-the-Father as binding together the triad Imaginary–Symbolic–Real). But here, the plot thickens, for there are more than one fatherly master-signifiers, such as the non-Israelis, the Isra-externalists, and the psycho-political fathers born in an illegitimate twist offspring of their sons and daughters, namely the chapters.

Let us then delve into this multiplied and self-multiplied dynamic in our preface, which is the very act of multiplication. It is belatedly pre-facing the book's structure and forming the relations of the chapters between their essayistic substance.

This definition of the psycho-political sprouted uniquely within the *substance* of the book chapters and not exteriorly by a master-author (as opposed to the notion of the author, which does not apply here, as the one who, like a gardener, professedly vegetates and sprouts what grows outside his vegetativeness by exterior watering, fertilization, and cultivation of the vegetative organism). The definition of the psycho-political has stemmed from the self-vegetative selfhood of the chapters and its self-growing seed as the word "thing." In this respect, the thing here signifies the logos as the stream of the word drawing to a seed significance, and as a concrete material thing, nucleolar and intractable (similar to how Lacan perceives the signifier as *an instance*). For us, this is the signifier of the psycho-political. This meta-vegetation then describes an interior spouting of the psycho-political within the essayistic domain that contains a covert internal desire that accompanies the self-determination toward the Israeli exteriority.

7   The ISRA-external teaches us that it is external also because it traverses the interiority of the Israeliness in its interiority, not just externally. Perhaps, the topology of the exterior and external may settle the tautological difficulty that the theory of (un)translatability has created for us in

relation to the notion of *the psycho-political*. Namely, instead of the dynamic in which the psychical undergoes political changes in its psychical, and the political undergoes psychical changes in its political, we could consider the psychical as what traverses the political and the political as what crosses the psychical, with each one of them allowing for itself a re-inscription of its identity. This traversing generates *a pre-tri-dimensional and post-two-dimensional* tautology in which the identical is unfathomably identical to itself.

How is it possible to explain the *two-and-a-half* dimension? Incidentally, this is a category in computer games, usually, regarding pseudo-triad positions expanded on a two-dimensional screen. In our context, it is a scandalous category that purports to explain the *scandal of writing* as a dimension that inscribes our lives, the dimension of the signifier that is found in the flat dimension of the bi-dimension, imaging for us our triadic lives, which is when the *in-between space* is generated, between the bi and the tri. Our lives swing between writing and our trinity. Then the tautology of the shift from the psychical itself to the psychical itself, when it fails to preserve itself as identical to itself, is possible by traversing the political within it. The same goes for the opposite, from the political to the political, when the traversing occurs as that additional dimension of the half, which is when the psychical leaps from one dimension to another. It is identical to itself but in another dimension (much like the Freudian tension between the conscious and the unconscious and their reciprocal translations, both the discursive and the mental, the pre-conscious embodying the two-and-a-half dimension. Perhaps, the conscious is to the unconscious like a leap to another dimension and vice versa. The preconscious that divides them performs the leap).

8   Perhaps, in the very motion of this vegetation within the Israeliness, from the innermost interior to the external horizon, may the psycho-political recognize its interior launching point between the psychical and the political. Namely, the explanation for the psycho-political tension here stems from the imagined exhibit constrained between the interior Israeliness in its exteriority, both from the exterior and crossing vertically. As we are about to examine, perhaps the tension between the political and the psychical has to do with the tension between these types of externalities and exteriorities, and the one that is split between the interior and this dual exterior one.

As disrupting as this may prove to be for the reader, the word uttering its honest selfhood here will further disrupt the order of things by asserting that this whole dynamic is inscribed retroactively for the chapters in question: from the preface engendering this exterior for them. The exterior externality that also topologically traverses the interiority, perhaps like the non-orientable surface of the Klein bottle, embodies itself in its negative reversibility or its negative formalization of the Klein bottle. It then embodies a marking of precisely the inaccessibility to knowledge in the reverse mode: where it is possible, there is no possibility, and where it is not possible, there is a possibility, a situation in which this mutual nullification renders a game of implied significance between the possible and the impossible, in a way unknown to the external reader. Only there is the knowledge to be found, namely in the actual ignorance of the reader who traverses the accustomed knowledge that does not contain, in fact, any real knowledge. However, even the one in the proximity of the information, the internal read, cannot traverse the knowledge close to him and access it simply.

9   From its inception, the definitional exhibition of the psycho-political that has been crystallized is in synchronicity with the historical events that took place in Israel during the last decade, events experienced by each one of the chapters in the interior encounter of the words within each chapter, in a way that these temporal events made these textual launching points touch. Out of the collision of the words with themselves and under the author's guidance, the echo of the histories infiltrated the bloodstream of the essayistic body. This echo crystallized how each chapter understood itself to have a psycho-political definition.

This self-definition stems from the self-inscription of the chapters for the author who is forced to assert what has yet to take shape in them, for they are an a priori void gradually filling up toward and for that primary void. He knows their filling, the one already found in their blockage, and executes it, including the terminology regarding the psycho-political present in that void, and on to the author and from there to the readers, like the ones being indirect to the author beyond any imaginings of the ideal reader, such as the territorial one. The being a reader **there**. Not **here**, for the here presumes knowing the primary void that engendered the chapters as if they were an accessible primary being, while the here is alien to the knowledge that the primary one is a void that fills up by virtue of the metaphysical and hermeneutic structure enveloping that void. The here needs to break off from its hereness through the thereness of the readers so that it may be recognized as the here.

10   What is the selfhood engendered by each one of the chapters that may be weighed as a single book? What is the anxiety whose meaning neither they nor their author knew? Nor did the anxiety know itself. What is that anxiety that extracted the self-definition of the chapters as psycho-political? As rationalistic and intelligible as this concept may seem, its conflictual terms, the psychical and the political, render it onerously obscure. For is there more of the current than the political, and is there more of the current than the psychical, and is there more evidence in the psychical, in the crazy political running around or in politicizing the psychical?

The case of the political being packed into the psychical and vice versa is probably what determined the decision – perhaps in haste but out of serious consideration on the part of the author – to have the chapters leap into one unifying book from the shoulders of the Israelis who themselves read in Hebrew straight on to an extra-territorial audience who themselves read in the English; language could be an opportunity for us to find ourselves through the reading, like the lake in which the waters of the territorial language are flushed in intimacy from the reader's mouth back to his/her eye without any possibility to get to know the interior stream of the lingual waters in the lake of language.

What is there in the encounter of the psychical with the political, as a subtle drive of the public endeavor that vibrates the interior truth of the territorial existence as it is intimately known to its subjects? Why has the internal decision been made for me that this subtle tremor will be first exported to the external ones? Perhaps because the slight tremor of the point of a meltdown between the psychical and the political requires open gaseous space, in which it may evaporate like intellectual perfume, rather than the steadiness of the local political rage that preserves it under the order of distress. The tremor of the space between the psychical and the political is precisely the sublime elevated from the territorial subjects. It needs a stage to perform for the exterior ones. It is a tremor that does not know itself, as is the stream of lingual waters that are interior to any language.

11 In the present preface, the elementarity is required to demonstrate its power, namely, to demonstrate the rudimentary elements of the book, the element – as its name indicates – not being divisible. There is division in its relations with other elements, not an interior one but between each element and the others, as if the intestines were exterior but still innermost and sensible to the body. The purpose of this configurational element in the preface is to bestow upon the readers that special, valuable element of their being readers, the space in which they exist, as well as the fundamental elements of the book with which they have a particular relationship, for they are visitors in these interior relations between the elements.

The presentation of the composition of the chapters as organizing the mapping of the rudimentary elements, as well as the self-presentation of the preface, lends the reader the possibility of an intimate reading under the consideration of element *warp* and element *weft* as metaphysical warp and weft (insofar as this logic locks the unity of reading with writing). In this reading, there is no linear gaze at the utterance toward a single **thesis** being inscribed at the expense of the interior-to-itself word, but a look at the weaving of the fabric, at the simultaneousness of the Persian fabric, to a certain extent – of the fractality of an ornament above another. Under the premise that distinguishes this metaphorical fabric from the real one, there is not one quilting point here from which the fabric is weaved, but innumerable launching or quilting points from which the reading may be weaved (this exhibit was brought up in a conversation with Yuval Barel whose painting features on the cover of *Critical Theology*, who mentioned the simultaneity of the gaze at the painting as opposed to the linearity of the written text, which for me does not represent writing).

12   The chapters that have been chosen for the readers outside of Israel, coming from the outside into the Israeli being – not necessarily because of their inability to read the chapters in Hebrew – touch upon the Israeli mentality. This compilation results from the yearning of the conceptual being of the psycho-political, a desire for Israeliness that engendered that being for the author who inscribes the chapters for themselves. A yearning, which is the act of writing and is in great danger of self-deterioration when it deviates from the textual workspace *on* the psycho-political *toward* the psycho-political being (then it starts to collapse because of the desire to neutralize the obscurity of the psycho-political in the direction of a single moment. This is also the space of the psycho-political game *onto*).

What is the justification for the decision that the chapters on the psycho-political traverse the Israeli being, and for which imagined exterior? Maybe it is because Israeliness, as a specific territorial, identical, or national being, represents the paradox of the psycho-political in the most acute fashion. This is the result of the acute psychical demonstrations of the political in the most emotional, affective way, while the interior psychical space of the Israelis is radically stamped by the political, which is either trauma-inducing or creates a pseudo-apolitical identity such as Mizrahi and Ashkenazi, or positions the subject under constant psychical stress due to the permanent interior state of emergency or conflict (the last two are slow-dancing close together and mutually agitating).

13   Perhaps, the psycho-political paradox in the Greek sense of the term *para-doksos* – *para* meaning *next to* and *doksos* – *road* or *opinion* – is a different structural form of the opinion or the idea or the trajectory, a sort of lateral walking along the wrong trajectory which will ultimately prove to be the right one. So, the psycho-political is the disruption of the path in the sense of inversion in which the political is psychical and the psychical is political. A struggle emerges when this concept reassumes the graphics of the connecting hyphen of the psycho-political thus far imagined, in which the psychical attaches itself to the political and vice versa. This is to say that each one is to be found in the heart of the other; each one is the truth or the essence of the other, to the point of conceitedly arguing that each one is the other. The psychical is in the nucleus of the political and the public, and the political is in the nucleus of the psychical in the most intimate

sense. In the sense that this dynamic exists in any compounded identity, it is also possible to describe the relationship between the psychical and the political as the formalization of the psychical as engulfed and the political as externalized belonging to the same essence or as an obscene side vis-à-vis a legitimate one, so that both sides embody each other's sides, and their contiguity is identical to the one between madness and ingenuity, an encounter between two substances separated only by a transparent, extremely thin cellophane. A flexible cellophane and any fluid acting on one side is flexibly embodied in the other. This contiguity may also be grasped via the Freudian hesitation, which consists of a drop of determination regarding the tension between the conscious and the unconscious, which entertain a permanent intimate encounter, like sexual intercourse between two partners. To some extent, the determined hesitation is expressed in the theoretical metaphor regarding the same tension between the conscious and the unconscious and their permanent contacts through conscious, pre-conscious, and unconscious baggage. The concept used by Freud to describe the relations between the system of the conscious and the pre-conscious and that of the unconscious is to be found in the title of chapter VI of the article "Unconscious": *Verkher der Beiden Systeme* ("The Interaction Between the Two Systems"). The German word *Verkehr* may be translated as communication, intersection, and traffic, but also as contiguity and intercourse. As aforementioned, the conceptual intercourse between these two mental systems is not only the purpose of Freud's theoretical presentation but also, discursively speaking, an instrument through which he may shape, describe, and support his own theoretical tension between hesitation and determination as two sides swaying in an intercourse dance on both sides of the fluidity separated by the cellophane. Perhaps this is also the explanation for the tension between the psychical and the political, as will be described as follows.

14   The chapters that the preface responds to their translation and their presentation to the ISRA-externalists have been composed during the last decade, with a few years' leap between them. These leaps were also the result of the meteoric surges within Israeli politics in the most psychical possible way. Radical changes that the psychical could not digest; the occurrence of one event permeating the next one, or whether it was war, civil protest, or conflict between political parties running for election. In effect, this very structure of the hierarchy of events *is* the unnerving psycho-political dynamic of the Israeli. Three of the chapters describe the political dynamic in Israel, but under a more precise axis than the political one, which is psycho-political in a hierarchical sense, in which the event abstains from its eventuality, as its political slides too rapidly into the psychical, namely is quickly translated into psychical, both in the sense of madness as well as in the mental-psychical sense, when the last two echo each other also

within an interior springboard in which one slides into the other. In any event, the dissolution of the political becomes effective or impetus, unable to contain the geometry of the power relations between all the players in the public arena. The geometry here is in the positive sense of a common disciplining toward the organization of the power relations in a geometrical manner that would prevent the power relation from becoming an actual power. Namely, they must remain on the level of the relational.

Then, into this configuration of events, the imaginary **few** are cast as volitional characters. This is a structure of scales upon scales in an intricate web of intercourse reciprocation that enables a personal imaginary settling down, which is seemingly independent, responsible, and intentional. But all these individual volitions creep into the intermediate gaps between the scales. To us, they seem independent. They are independent insofar as there are gaps that enable them to act.

In all the chapters, in one form or another, there is in the background a dominant figure in Israeli politics during those years, the prime minister of Israel, Benyamin Netanyahu. Even though it may not be necessary to introduce him to the non-Israeli readers, it may still be worthwhile to introduce them to the Israeli psycho-political dynamic in general and Netanyahu's modes of interaction within this dynamic. One of the chapters even argues that Netanyahu is, in fact, the essence of this dynamic.

15   The present word is one in the sense of it being in an individual encounter with the reader, thus bringing all its sisters together to the bundle of words in the present article, and it is singular at any given moment, albeit not specific; it is one word at a time, and as such, it attempts to capture the wordiness of the word itself. Thus, it is a priori demonstrating the dilemma surrounding the question of the psycho-political – how a general public sphere exists at all – in an attempt to word the words that have been compiled in three of the chapters. Word in the sense of their demonstration, while they amass as words describing a psycho-political situation, so that the word here sustains the mode of their wordiness in each one of the chapters, and the way they communicate with each other.

These modes of operation allude to the psycho-political situationality or hierarchiality in the sense that it is there where the tension between the psychical and the political (as aggressive) is created, a tension that is itself the tension of wording the mentality toward the power relations and vice versa. The mentality here refers to the collective psyche, but also the private one assembled in the private. This is not about the psychology of the masses but about examining the public sphere as a political metaphysical coming into being, in which the power relations themselves are the collective psyche. The political here is the formalization of power, not necessarily in the violent sense, but in an act vis-à-vis power as a potential of express-ing the relations between factors. This is a potential of intentional coming into being. Namely, the political is what transpires in the space of relations (and not necessarily the power relations driven by power; the same relation of *a* to its others).

16   The word perceives itself out of a European linguistic inscription of the Greek logos as *word*, and from there back to the Greek as the coming into being of the being itself as conversing with its own logic, and now with the political logic, in which Israel conducts itself under the thingness of reality in which various **inter**-political powers stream along, while the **inter** is what is assigned imaginary or imaging devolutions to the point where actuality has lost all remnants of the image.

The preface attempts to offer the non-Israeli readers a belated explana-tion, albeit introductory. An overdue consideration, even if perhaps ele-mentary, acting as a hallway to the rest of the rooms in the apartment, in what concerns the author's political as well as psychical state of mind; one author who is also three different authors. But it also explains the words themselves that address those readers in all their exteriority, while the bor-der of their exteriority between their Israeliness and their own being is the vibrating thing yearning for some recognition of that Israeliness. This kind of vibration requires particular scrutiny, enabling a reverberating gaze back on the Israelis from an external sphere, not completely external but also exterior to me from within the interiority of this circular movement.

The word treads carefully, following its own paths within the Hebrew in fear and trembling of the reality it reacts to and from and within and for, towards the external. It does so while deploying the reality of this existence as the space of inter-political tensions, namely between several forms of the political as forms, *idea* – ideas or metaphor in the Greek sense, or in the German sense of *Vorstellung* – demonstration or presentation or image. But the demonstration is not a representation of what it is not itself, an aspect of the *demonstration itself*, but the image as demonstration is itself an idea, such as a political one juggling within the interior relations between itself and other images and images of the neighboring political ideas, such as the ones tackled in this collection: Mizrahi, Ashkenazi, Netanyahu, and protest. This inter-political compound of relations itself contains consecutive or background images such as monarchy, democracy, and others. Then, it is possible to understand the political as comprising two different levels of political ideas. Still, there exists the danger of con-fusing the two levels: the level of ideas, which is an image to itself, and that of the background idea that mediates between them and the actual reality, as it were. Isn't this a metaphorical expansion as well?

17 The three demonstrations of **the Mizrahiness, the protest, and Netanyahu**
render themselves in the present chapters as an effort on the part of the
word whose ghost still haunts this preface in pursuit of *the Ding* within it.
This effort aims to construct a theoretical knowledge, both foolish as well
as enabling[6] (an almost nonsensical or Don Quixotish but quite a strenu-
ous effort to promote something toward an uncertain end), which could
carry the burden of the psycho-political occurrences, whose psychical has
been inundated by the political and vice versa. Following is the dynamic of
the three categories:

The Mizrahiness. From the moment it was published in the Israeli journal,
Theory and Criticism, the chapter concerned with this topic aroused both
increasing curiosity and appreciation for its boldness as well as resentment
on the part of Mizrahi theoreticians and activists claiming that the author
has disrobed them of their justified position as victims and that his perception is ostensibly a-historical and even in denial of history. Apart from the
fact that in question is an autobiographical theory that comes to terms with
the problem of the author's personal identity, perhaps even as an allegory
for the situation as a whole, it is, of course, possible to debate the validity
of these arguments; the author insists on the following two responses:

1 A refusal to automatically adopt the status of the victim (be it a theore-
   tician investigating the Mizrahi or a Mizrahi in relation to him/herself
   and others of the exact origin), namely, apply the status to the sufferer
   in a simplistic way without assigning any responsibility to him/her for it.
2 A refusal to automatically adopt the implications of the past on the
   present as a one-way direction.

For us, Mizrahiness is a demonstration in the sense that it represents the
thing that represents itself as the representation of the thing (in contiguity
with the Freudian *Wortvorstellung*), which represents the act of representation (not the word tomato > (meaning) tomato but the word tomato >
representation of the word tomato), like a machine that engenders itself
out of its very discursive activity or out of its self-reference with no other
meaning. This issue is manifested in the very existence of the current
polemics regarding the historical "origin" of Mizrahiness: is it a constitution of the name or/and the identity conferred by the state or the community known as Mizrahi? Being a self-demonstration with no meaning
outside its self-agitation and the polemics surrounding it positions, the
Mizrahiness is in two psycho-political axes: the political space as psychical
and as being included in the psychical and the psychical as political and as
being included in the political.

In the first axis, the very debate on whether this is a constitution of identity conferred by the state, by Zionism, by the Ashkenazi elite, or by the
Mizrahi community itself demonstrates precisely the dynamic in which the

Mizrahi is but a signifier floating beyond (or under) the state; a semi-political interim space that as such enables the political manipulation of the seeming non-political for specific interests.

The other axis is the demonstration being embodied entirely in the logic of **the tautology of identity**, starting with that of the rigorous scholar covered in ivory,[7] and ending with the ordinary people whom we imagine as common when they are not common at all, albeit their efficient use of various "reasons" and "explanations." We refer to the logic that tends to fall into the trap of the **Mizrahi is Mizrahi**, or into its sub-tautology the **Mizrahi is Arab**. We point to these matters to underscore how, in the amorphous psycho-political space, in which the political and the psychical contaminate each other, there is neither an exact nor a stable position for the political formula of identity. And this is precisely what enables the political and the manipulation within it. A manipulation that leaps from the amorphous psycho-political plane straight onto the ontological field (where there is a real, comforting response that stabilizes identity and a professed solution to the self-representation of the demonstration is found) because – as the chapter shows – the present concretely recreates the past, at least insofar as the identity and its axis of victimization are concerned. This is not to say that there was no oppression in the past, but that the oppression exists in **past-present** persistent synchronicity that inscribes the past as an event separated from the present somewhere in the year 5555, thereby engendering a separate substance that constitutes the reason for the beings. At the same time, the direction is no less inverse.

18   As far as the **protest** is concerned, here as well, the diffusions, the confusion, and the obscurity were what enabled the political manipulation of the protests and the same thing that caused the Tent Protest to dissolve. It might even be that the psycho-political chapter before us is part of the same logic, and we say this because of the preface that aspires to assess and observe itself as a defining preface.

As for **Netanyahu**, we have here an inversion, his psycho-political dimension being exact and not in the least amorphous. It drove people to join together in one of two camps: the "only Bibi" camp or the "just not Bibi" one. Furthermore, the dimension of the imaginary fixation almost took over the political arena. At least one side of the Israeli political sphere knew how to evade this psycho-political dynamic, and through the inversion (in the Lacanian sense, *envers*, which is not a reversal but a lateral inversion), neutralize this same deficiency.

19   These dynamics might imply that precisely the external gaze of non-Israelis or Israelis, when exterior to themselves, could offer an insight into the psycho-political formalization of the Israeli pandemonium, since the lack of intimate knowledge of these themes is precisely what could tap into their being nebulous themes disguised as solid stars in the Israeli skies of anxiety.

Moreover, the book chapters are caught up in a strange topological relation in which the factor running around is Netanyahu. The Tent Protest discussed in the respective chapter occurred during the period of Netanyahu's government and was identified as an "Ashkenazi" protest, while "Mizrahiness" is identified with Netanyahu's supporters. In both cases exists a sociological obnubilation regarding the identity of the communities, as is reflected in the Hebrew term "mishtaknez" (a Mizrahi who has adopted an Ashkenazi aroma and is consequently considered fraudulent). In this respect, Netanyahu is a **cutting signifier** that enables a defining cut between these obscure identities, making contiguous use of signifiers such as Jewish, right-wing, national, and traditional. The left has swiftly fallen into this trap since it has been afflicted by the distress of this obscurity, which it shares as well.

As we have pointed out concerning the question of translation, the obscurities within the psycho-political substances are also the result of the formalization that places entity **a** at the base of entity **b** that only re-expresses itself as **b** (for **b** equals **b**). And the psycho-political as an affective occurrence of the political order is driven by self-persuasion regarding the psychic exclusivity of a single factor (which is, in fact, within its other). Thus, for example, we need to comprehend the Ashkenazi from within the Mizrahi and vice versa. But both of them are imaginary, including each one's interiority in the other. And then comes another entanglement when this whole dynamic creates another conceptual obscurity—hence the psycho-political attempt to cut through this mess. When writing these chapters, the **knife** has a name – Netanyahu. Or Bibi. And it is still sharp.

Itzhak Benyamini
February 17th, 2022

Note

1 Walter Benjamin, "The Task of the Translator.", Ibid, p. 259.

Chapter 1

Introduction

The Citizen Crushing under the Political Entanglement

This book is a succession of eight critical psycho-political chapters on the reality in Israel during the last two decades, an attempt to present a critical analysis, which is a kind of political autobiography, of me as a citizen. The analysis itself is also a theoretical testimony to my political experience within the democratic movement in the sense that the very attempt to analyze my experience and that of my fellow-fighters and attach a meaning in a Sisyphean manner to a totally illogical situation in itself constitutes a performance of the political-emotional or the psycho-political experience of the civil-democratic movement, which in its futile struggle to preserve democracy is attempting to understand its situation and the struggle itself, without possessing any theoretical tools while groping its way through this political entanglement. Therefore, this is not so much an analysis of the situation, but rather a meditation on the very attempt to retrieve some theoretical tools. In this sense, it is both a theoretical and a meta-theoretical analysis construed in a synchronic and complementary manner. As if Aristotle were writing concurrently his *Physics* and his *Metaphysics* using the very same words, and not in two successive, separate works. The very metaphysical analysis is also what endows the physical itself with meaning and not only the theoretical questions pertaining to the analysis.

This very twist, this structure, is my methodological course, as well as the very object of the critical course. A theoretical twist that is an allegory to my emotional entanglement as a citizen. A twist that is consequently ensnared in a succession of wordiness, which at times might be truly hard to understand, as I strive to elucidate the theoretical-critical experience in attempting to make some sense out of a hallucinatory political situation. And so, the theoretical strive cannot be separated from my own self-reflection regarding the theoretical and the meta-political attempt to retrieve some theoretical, conceptual tools for analyzing the situation. It is a philosophical reflection of an emotional state of despair and futility regarding the effort to attain a general comprehension of the civic status within the movement, fighting for democratic life in Israel, when it is experienced as an increasing submergence of the subject into the dunghill of a horrific political deadlock.

DOI: 10.4324/9781003667339-1

The chapters represent a written testimony of several significant stages in my writing regarding the continuous disaster that has befallen Israel during the years of Benyamin Netanyahu's regime. It might be possible to retrospectively understand the writing of this disaster as what had been holding an unconscious cognizance that all the characteristics of this perilous space would be ultimately channeled into one catastrophic future gist – October 7. Namely, the meta-theoretical character of the discussion very likely possessed along the way some interior, covert knowledge of the fact that this entangled situation would only expand and intensify toward a moment of total collapse, even of the very entanglement itself.

This unconscious recognition, which may be identified only in retrospect, regarding a continuous political disaster leading to a specific political disaster – a disaster whose brutality stems from its being continuous and even deterministic-tendentious, and a disaster whose brutal characteristic is its intolerable momentariness – originates from the fact that this whole progression is linked to a single specific person. The center of fabrication of the political tension in Israel is Benyamin Netanyahu, the one who has served, is serving, and no one can predict how long will continue to serve, as the Prime Minister of Israel. Even if we cannot pin on him the entire responsibility for all the social and political maladies in Israel, the very fact that both the right and the left are ensnared in a trap of either identifying with his politics or opposing it positions him under the heavy burden of liability regarding that disastrous progression; for all the public institutions, from the army to the last of the public schools, have been collapsing into a hole of futility and corruption, while their leader is busy destroying the State mechanisms, notably the guardians of the Law, so that he himself may escape several judicial instances related to his acts of corruption.

It follows that the dynamics of a catastrophic progression leading to a momentary catastrophe, which is a converging point, has brought about the most brutal, ferocious, and insane attack on the citizens of Israel: the moment in which the Hamas members crossed over the fences and all the military and the defense forces failed to provide protection to the citizens who were so brutally exposed to the engulfment of the *Real*. And the traumatic Real is both the unfathomable acts of plunder, rape, butchery, and abduction committed by the Hamas and other Palestinians who joined them, as well as the very exposure to a situation in which there is no possibility of defense, no defending big Other.

This breaking point continues its progression into another mode of catastrophe, in which on the one hand the Hamas has brought on the Palestinians their greatest disaster since the 1948 Nakba, distancing them even farther from the possibility of a sound solution to end the Israeli occupation and establish a Palestinian State alongside Israel; on the other hand, Israel and its citizens are prey to anti-Semitic attacks throughout the globe, from Columbia University to Teheran. In question is a multifaceted complex of disaster in which the collapse is mutual on both sides of the fence. In this disastrous situation, the fascist forces on both sides strive toward achieving hatred of the other side, which would drag the entire region into a radical solution of annihilating the enemy. This disastrous vanishing point embodied in the Hamas attack on the Jewish settlements along the Gaza Envelope led to Israel's counterattack on Hamas. Currently, while these lines are written, multitudes of protestors outside the Israel–Palestine territories, voice their support of the Palestinian struggle without in the least being aware of the crisis situations in both the Israeli and the Palestinian spaces. Within both these spaces, there are ongoing power struggles among various political, religious, and national groups and conceptions.

Naturally, no society is monolithic, and all political space holds interior unbridgeable tensions. Such are both the Israeli space as well as the Palestinian one, each one in itself, as well as the space of the Arab–Israeli or the Jewish–Muslim conflict. The concept "conflict" must be understood in a multidimensional way, not as an axis of conflict between two monolithic entities but rather as a *complex* holding a multiplicity of conflicts within each one of them, and that the space of the interior conflicts on the one side is in conflict with the interior conflicts of the other.

A more precise description of this complex may be found in the Freudian concept of "over-determination" (or "multiple determination"). The concept describes the complex relation between the raw materials of the dream drama and the end products of its various components, a relation so deeply complex and ramified that it is virtually impossible to reduce the dream to a single coherent signification. Through this concept, Freud not only proposes a theoretical significance for the dream but also seeks to understand his own experience as an interpreter of the dream, while being at his wit's end vis-à-vis the unresolvable entanglement of the dream and its origins. First and foremost, Freud's conceptualization reflects the analyst's own distress in attempting to decipher the dream conundrum. But since any person awakening from a dream is also in the capacity of an interpreter, this conceptualization may also account for her/his experience and for the dream itself (which it too, in its hallucinatory state, attempts to ascribe meaning to the emotional distress of the dreamer).

Along these lines, it may be possible to describe the nightmare of the Israeli–Palestinian conflict, and the attempt to assign it meaning and suggest a possible resolution. The conflict does not rest solely on the axis of the Occupation nor on the axis of religion or democracy, but rather on a multiplicity of these axes. Each one of these axes, describing the encounter of a factor from one side with a factor from the other side, branches out each time into several factors. My own experience is also situated in this entanglement in which, on the one hand as a citizen of this country, I feel a part of it and obligated to defend it vis-à-vis its enemies and antagonists; on the other hand, in addition to the enemies from without there are no less dangerous ones from within that compromise the future and safety of my country. Such is the current leadership, with its scheme to do away with democracy and its total disregard of any

possibility of making peace with our neighbors. In this entanglement of identification, I personally find myself in a multifaceted logic of identification,
including my own encounter with another citizen of this country, when a succession of my own identifications encounters his/hers. (Also, within the interior tensions of the Palestinian cultural fabric, of which I do not feel licensed
to speak, but just briefly remark that there exists a large number of Arabs and
Palestinians, e.g., members of religious, national, or gender minorities, who do
not necessarily support the fascist Hamas movement.)

What nevertheless might be the central axis in what seems to be an unresolvable entanglement, impossible to untangle? There are two axes that seem to unite
into a central one: a monolithic firm grasp of the land and anti-democracy.
Or, in other words, religious and anti-occidental nationalism. Here – Jewish
nationalism; there – Islamist nationalism. The depiction of these interior political tensions in Israel, the identification or nonidentification with them, might
help both the non-Israeli readers as well as the resisting forces in this turmoil
to understand that the struggle is not necessarily between Israel and Palestine,
but rather between the fascist forces and those who support progress, modern-
ization, and the promotion of equality and freedom among individuals in both
nations.

The Israeli political space oscillates between properties of responsibility and
arbitrariness, between a deep true feeling of belonging and the feeling of alienation and loss of way, and between the willingness to reconcile with the Arabs
and end the Occupation and the disregard for the Palestinians' suffering and
their oppression; but the main lingering feelings are severe onerousness and
anxiety induced by the political deadlock. These feelings, both justified and
unjustified, are cynically and politically exploited.

This book represents the various stages in a continuous, onerous narrative
that is my life as a concerned but also committed citizen in a country both
dejected and dejecting but also powerful and empowering of its citizens, at
least the Jewish ones. As a Jewish Israeli, I am well aware of my dominance,
which may exist at the expense of the non-Jewish minorities, but within this
privilege too, there are various shades. Insofar as I understand the relations
between these different levels of dominance – and the disparities between religious and secular Jews, between Ashkenazi and Sephardi Jews, and between
the various communities within the Muslim and the Arab space in Israel – they
reflect a political metaphysics that within the experience of being Israeli suc-
cumbs each one of these groups to various degrees of anxiety vis-à-vis the lives
of the others.

In probing these various degrees of both personal and collective anxiety,
whether justified or not, I have used methodological tools that Freud and
Lacan have offered me. Notably, the insight of anxiety being the positioning of
subjectivity against the nonexistence of the object of the *Real*. Throughout the
years, my understanding has deepened around two historical pivots. On the
one hand, the depth of anxiety regarding the Real, on the other, the depth of

its exploitation. I have expressed this through my neologism, "the psycho-political." This concept, more than it aims to speak about the connection between the two moments, speaks about a collision, or more precisely, about a border that is becoming increasingly blurred in contemporary Israel, and perhaps in other political systems around the world. Political systems in which the political permeates the personal too instantaneously and too personally through social media, which on the one hand produce more committed citizens but on the other, stand firm in their unidimensional politics, whether conservative populist or leftist populist.

In a way, the task of this book is not necessarily to effect accessibility to the complexity of the political situation in Israel, but rather to manifest it, perhaps as a response to those who perceive the Israeli society in a monolithic fashion and are not aware of the various tensions within it and of the ongoing struggle for democracy.

The preface to the book is a meta-theoretical chapter that was written about a few years ago to foreword the German edition of the book and is an attempt to perceive the translation's position as an impossibility, echoing my feelings at the time that a written representation of the Israeli experience for non-Israelis is virtually impossible. It is rather a tortuous, complex piece attesting to a form of theoretical failure to explain even to myself the meaning of my political situation as a citizen. For in these chapters, I searched for the "right" words to describe my own frustration with my life in Israel as a citizen, how we are getting farther and farther away from a possible political solution to the Israeli–Palestinian conflict, and how the political and democratic culture is washing away from beneath us. Thus, while searching for the right words, these texts meander restlessly through political, philosophical, sociological, and psychoanalytical theories and concepts, in order to retrieve some sound conceptualization for the experience of anxiety in the face of the Real, as conceptualized by Lacan. Here, a political Real.

The second chapter of the book is a conceptual background to the understanding of the citizen's abjectivation and anxiety. It explores the foundational entanglement between the citizen and the concept of the political, focusing on the processes of abjectivation and negativation as intrinsic mechanisms in the constitution of political subjectivity. Drawing on Aristotle's definition of the polis and its derivatives, and expanding through a psychoanalytical and philosophical framework inspired by Freud, Lacan, Kristeva, Hegel, Heidegger, Foucault, Agamben, and Althusser, the chapter critically examines how the citizen is constituted not through mere subjugation or affiliation with the State, but through a deeper ontological condition of non-non-affiliation, not oppositional but structural, marking the subject as inherently situated within and against the symbolic order that defines the political. This logic is extended to contemporary Israel, in that it identifies how political subjectivity is shaped by competing dynamics of self-abjection, victimhood, and ideological identification within the State-supra-subject. Ultimately, the chapter challenges the fantasy of political liberation, arguing instead for a deconstructive approach that destabilizes the conceptual space of the political and exposes its dependence on abjectivation. The citizen, then, is not merely a legal entity but a metaphysical construct ensnared in perpetual oscillation between belonging and rejection – both a product and object of the political itself.

The third chapter is related to a social protest that occurred at the outset of Netanyahu's regime. It describes the revolt of the liberal segments in Israel, which are stereotypically identified as secular and Ashkenazi. The chapter employs the Freudian concept of the Uncanny (the unhomely) to demonstrate the sense of alienation within the homely, felt by the protesters at the beginning of Netanyahu's regime. This sense of losing the homely and the onerousness of nonexistence will keep on intensifying.

The fourth chapter elaborates on this motif through the concept of "the anxiety of Israeliness," which is an attempt – inspired by the thought of Freud, Lacan, and Heidegger – to understand Netanyahu's tactics to reinvent the Israeli *Real*, while cultivating the feelings of onerousness and anxiety in the average Israeli.

In the fifth chapter on the Mizrahi Israeli, I discuss the way in which Netanyahu and his associates devoted this tactics to reconstitute the identity of Mizrahi Jews to the point of constituting the equation in which Bibist = Mizrahi.

The sixth chapter on the ontology of political time discusses the frustration of the democratic movement, determined to fight against the determinism of the "judicial self-coup" on its part, determined to do away with democracy in Israel by using democratic means, prior to October 7.

The seventh chapter was written following October 7, and is an attempt to understand this event under the concept of Netanyahu's anxiety machine, along the lines of thought presented in the book as a whole; the way through which Netanyahu's demagogy and toxic machine of the media that has been recruited to voice his politics, echo and reecho, time and again, the reconstitution of the "proper identity of the Israeli," as being conflated with supporting him in his annulment of democracy.

The eighth chapter is a lecture I held during a seminar on continental philosophy, whose topic this year was philosophy under war. In a way, it represents a kind of closure, positioning my thought at a point that cuts between the political and the theological. The first chapter explored the Gordian Knot between these two aspects. But throughout my experience as a citizen under the "judicial self-coup" and takeover of Israel by the nationalist right-wing forces, I attempted to think of the category of "You" as being cut off from the temptation to position it in any relation with the theological. There is no sexual relation between the You and God, if I may be allowed to paraphrase Lacan's formula regarding the nonexistence of sexual relations.

Within this political Real, the structure producing the feeling of anxiety, which escapes simple lingual articulation, is a topological structure of an entanglement which cannot be untangled; any attempt to untangle or break free from it only reinforces it and the sense of suffocation within it. Such is the experience of fighting against Netanyahu. The more its opposition grows, his influence seems to both diminish and grow stronger, which produces the onerousness in relation to this aporetic political suffocation. And while this paradox may be expressed herewith through words, it is devoid of any logic: how can something weaken and simultaneously grow stronger? What is also uncanny is that Netanyahu is but one person, a single entity, while we are referring to the entire system of the Israeli State, to the Israeli–Palestinian conflict, and to Democracy in Israel.

Hence, how can it be that, on the one hand, there exists an extremely complex entanglement, and on the other, we can pinpoint a particular element? One explanation is that Netanyahu has been making use of all of Israel's and Zionism's internal fallacies in order to manipulate and further reinforce this internal contradictory situation, while various factors see in him the omnipotent deliverer who will resolve all these internal contradictions. Or, they are using him to serve their own agendas. Netanyahu is a sort of Lacanian Name-of-the-Father, encompassing the whole entangled organization of the topological registers of the political and security systems in Israel. Not only does he organize the relations between the registers he is also continuously and directly producing them: The Israeli Imaginary, the Symbolic, and the Real. Ironically, his opponents are even more enmeshed in this entanglement, for in respect to some of his opponents, for example, in the religious Zionist party, it may be argued that they themselves manipulate this topology. In the case of the Mizrahi Israelis, the extent to which Netanyahu is shaping their consciousness and the extent to which they are manipulating the topology of reality under the assumption that they control him to benefit them is unclear. If we can identify an entangled dialectic of mutual exploitation between Bibi and his supporters that affects the shaping of the topology in Israel, perhaps within it the most "dominated" ones are his opponents, whose entire political design and horizon revolves around putting an end to his dominating them. In this predicament, the left in Israel is cornered into a position which is to some extent, as outrageous as it may sound – Bibist!

Only time will tell whether Benyamin Netanyahu will be victorious in his project of ruining Israel and putting an end to its Zionism, Judaism, and democracy.

Chapter 2

The Non-Non-Affiliation of the Citizen to the Political

Conceptual Background to the Citizen's Abjectivation and Anxiety

1

My aim is not to reinstate a novelty – neither new nor old – but rather to make present what is already made present in the political realm, understood in its transhistorical configuration. It is this presence that unfolds along a temporal axis as marked by the perpetual return of the concept's eternal recurrence. Such recurrence emerges from the conceptuality of "the political" as it was born in Greek thought, including the original fallacies that accompanied its genesis, fallacies which are also key to the space of action within it.

Aristotle states:

ὅτι μὲν οὖν ἡ πόλις καὶ φύσει πρότερον ἢ ἕκαστος, δῆλον: εἰ γὰρ μὴ αὐτάρκης ἕκαστος χωρισθείς, ὁμοίως τοῖς ἄλλοις μέρεσιν ἕξει πρὸς τὸ ὅλον, ὁ δὲ μὴ δυνάμενος κοινωνεῖν ἢ μηδὲν δεόμενος δι' αὐτάρκειαν οὐθὲν μέρος πόλεως, ὥστε ἢ θηρίον ἢ θεός.
(Aristotle, *Politica*, 1.1253a, 25)[1]

It is clear, then, that the city [*polis*] both exists by nature and is prior in nature to the individual. For if an individual is not self-sufficient when separated, he will be in a similar state to that of the other parts in relation to the whole. And anyone who cannot live in a community with others, or who does not need to because of his self-sufficiency, is no part of a city, so that he is either a wild beast or a god.[2]

This statement captures the figure of the citizen within the concept of the political, with its entire historical and textual aura. Yet, as I will attempt to show, this concept itself is ensnared in a Freudo-Lacanian logic of the subject's birth within the symbolic order, which also places the subject in an eternal gap, excluded from the symbolic itself.

This sort of mapping seeks to expose the peeping tail folded within the concealment of the conceptual fabric of the political. I will call it the act of *Abjectivation*. It is an act that stems from the conceptual space of the political. To it, I will attach its accompanying mechanism: *negativation*. Abjectivation will be understood as the practice of charging the subject with humiliating and debasing significations, and negativation as a radical act of denial that does

DOI: 10.4324/9781003667339-2

not necessarily refer to any specific characterizations of the subject. In fact, in question is the fusion of the structural component of negativation and the content component of abjectivation. Each one of them contains something of the other: abjectivation negativates and negativation abjectivates, especially from the vantage point of the subject which experiences these acts upon its own "flesh."

2

Since the focus here is on the conceptual fabric of the political subject – a field in which everything is entangled to the point that it is no longer possible to distinguish professional from personal sources – the modes of their expressions in thought at this stage will defer the discussions regarding the various conceptual movements of each and every thinker constantly amalgamated within the conceptual space. The following mapping of the political is charted within this philosophical space, which is both a reference and an object of inquiry. In particular, I refer to thinkers related to the tradition of continental thought: Hegel, Heidegger, Lacan, Kristeva, Foucault, Agamben, and Althusser.

Specifically, I focus on Aristotle and Lacan, whose works provide the principal threads through which my discourse is woven: Aristotle, in his trajectory from "jouissance" to institutional signifier; Lacan, in his recourse from the signifier back to "jouissance" and what he refers to as the subject situated outside the object in the process of objectifying.

Aristotle and Lacan, with and within Hegel, and Hegel within them, constitute the architecture of the thought of mastery and servitude. I leap over this conceptual stage so that we may encounter the figure of the citizen who is not born out of the dialectics of subjugation – that is, from a relation to a master or a State – but rather from a position of non-affiliation altogether, and thus from non-affiliation with the State. This is not a negation of an authoritarian factor, but rather a negation of what cannot, in effect, be negated: in question is the subject's indifference to the political and to the State, as implied in Aristotle's remark, not an opposition but rather the subject's natural and inherent non-affiliation.

3

I aim to explore the *anxiety of the political* in general and in Israel in particular, by performing a discursive recourse to the practice of *abjectivation*, which is part and parcel of the very constitution of the political subject in the course of its negativation and the negativation of its negativation.[3]

Both Freud[4] and Schmitt[5] formulate a tenacious and urgency-ridden position regarding the subject and the State, historically valid in the sense that it captures the mode through which the subject is presented as being constituted, namely, the subject exists merely as the presentation of the mode of its constitution. Indeed, both Freud and Schmitt demonstrate that the political and the psychic systems alike create the subject through an initial detection of an external force or enemy, which is the negative of the internal good and the source from which the internal good is generated retrospectively by way of negativation of the external and evil negative.

Furthermore, in Aristotle's case – and possibly in line with the etymology of the word *polis* – it is the external that defines the external as evil. Then comes negativation, the need to mark it as external or hostile, followed by repression as an internalized form of negativation or as abjectivation. Then begins the phase of negation – which is, in effect, already the negation of the negativation – followed by the negation of the negating negation.

I follow here Freud's understanding of the originary politica – the *Ur*-politica – as a construction internal to the subject, which constitutes external–internal relations which, in turn, constitute this politica and the subject in mutually constitutive relations. The very discursive understanding of Freud is in mutually constitutive relations with the discursive or the philosophical-political dimension of the *Mind (Geist)*, in the Hegelian sense, which informs the understanding of the concept "political." Freud's understanding of the subject under the concept of the political is in mutually constitutive relations with the understanding of the political, so that his conception of the subject is also the product of the conception of the political as an emergency-ridden mechanism within internal–external relations.

Moreover, Freud's conception may sharpen for us the angle of the subject's precedence and its internal–external relations, as well as its implications on the political and the State, ostensibly in opposition to the supposition that the political relation to the internal–external and subsequently to the subject begins with the State or the political, for example, as it is presented by Agamben in his Heideggerian ontology[6] regarding the Being and the State. Even if our understanding of this inception in the Freudian sense is a retroactive invention of the political, we are situated here in a sort of textual immanence (possibly a diffusion between Agamben and Freud), where the relations between Freud's position and Agamben's are not in opposition but rather in simultaneous proximity-distance, such as the immense nearness and the immense and infinite remoteness between those holding the two sides of the same coin: great contiguity alongside inaccessibility.

Both for Freud and Agamben, in question is the intricacy of the becoming of the subject, of the State, and of the political and the determination of which precedes which. Furthermore, this whole movement is trapped within a global subjectivity, or a global *Geist*, ignorant of the distinction between the subject and the political. To clarify the distinction, it is possible to draw on the metaphor regarding the Freudian conceptualization: for Freud, the subject holds within it various components, one of which is *das Ich* – the "I" – which oddly enough also represents the self-subject in its generality.

Similarly, discursive components here, such as the discursive element in Freud or in Agamben, can be interwoven with one another. Each one of the thinkers conceptualizes the subject and the political through strange topologi-cal configurations, where the totality A contains various components, includ-ing component A itself.

And if such an intricacy exists, it is perceived as unbearable. Perhaps Agamben's scheme can be read as a romantic desire to escape these entangle-ments between the subject and the sovereign political. All this is heading toward a messianic futurity, which albeit an unrealized fantasy, for the subject still holds the promise for liberation and transcendence. In opposition to this fantasy, the inclination toward the Freudian variable of the equation prompts me to insist that the political as discourse may have been born in Greece, but guilt – foundational guilt – is much more archaic and essential: the source of guilt lies in the simultaneity of the subject constituting the *Symbolic* order (in the Lacanian sense) and the Symbolic order constituting the Subject. In this view, the *Real* is precisely this double foundation of the Symbolic and the Subject, which also constructs the fantasy of a point of origin that escapes the tension between politicization and anti-politicization, as a labyrinth in which Agamben is trapped.

4

Following Chantal Mouffe's distinction between *the political* and *politics*,[7] or Jean-Luc Nancy's between *le politique* and *la politique*,[8] I attempt to propose a similar distinction, focusing on the former. *The political* as a concept is self-referential; it determines its characteristics, its conceptuality, and its very being; a philosophical concept imbued with historical residues, but it is also a concept that describes the structurality of the space it describes: the correspondent of the symbolic order (the order of conceptuality as structurality). In this sense, *the political* is: (a) the depiction of the horizontal encounter between various subjects, (b) the depiction of the vertical relation between that horizontal encounter and what I term "the Supra-subject" (such as the State).

This conceptuality is closely related to the Greek network of signifiers, that is its direct derivative: *polis* (the city, the state, *polités* (the citizen of the *polis*), *politika* (politics, the affairs of the *polis*, the science of politics as *politikē epistēmē*, and the title of Aristotle's text), *politikos* (the civic, the political), *politeia* (constitution, citizens' rights, as well as title of Plato's and Aristotle's texts regarding *Athens' constitution*), and *politeuma* (governance).

5

Furthermore, through the concept, I attempt to touch upon its etiology in order to resuscitate the dead metaphor that has become a concept in the process of externalizing its metaphysical surplus. Reviving the dead meta-phor through its partial preservation as a conceptual metaphor may resonate here with a broader attempt to awaken from slumber the dead metaphors of *the political* and *the civic* – in the sense of *politēs* – insofar as they are constitutive of the conceptual space. This is a space the birth of which is concurrent with that of the metaphor as well as with its death in the word indicating the Greek *fortified city*, and the subsequent *polis*. Etymological dictionaries trace the word's origin to the essence of the Greek *polis* as "citadel, fort, city," a meaning also found in the Proto-Indo-European language – "citadel; enclosed space, often on high ground; hilltop" – and in Sanskrit.[9]

Immanent in this etiology are its geographical conditions: a fortified, elevated segment around which the city was built, such as the Acropolis in ancient Athens or the Temple Mount in Jerusalem. Thus, the political, in its original physical sense, is linked with an elevated, inaccessible space, separating its inhabitants from those who do not inhabit it and whose status is obviously inferior, even in the most literal sense of the word. Even prior to its death, the metaphor is fundamentally linked to corporeality in the most physical sense. From this perspective, metaphysics is a metaphorical elevation from the physical toward the conceptual abstract.

6

By contrast, politics seems to extract itself from this conceptual and metaphorical structurality of the political. Politics is the imaginary and narrative reduction of the symbolic-conceptual structurality, as embodied in the daily life of the spirit of history, a reduction of a symbolic-conceptual structurality to a personal dimension. Politics generates this reduction through the movement from the subject's space to that of organizations and personae: parties, ideologies, members of parliament, prime ministers, and party functionaries. Ultimately, we are faced with the coupling of the symbolic and the imaginary, and subsequently with the third order termed by Lacan *the Real* (*le Réel*). Notwithstanding, it is not possible to withdraw from the metaphysical to the physical, nor from the metaphorical-conceptual to the corporeal, as we are already within a conceptual mode of existence. Politics is therefore imaginary-figurative and not corporeal-tangible, as the imaginary itself is also a textual mode, existing beyond corporeality, an image of the corporeal. Hence, in question is the textual reality of the body in politics.

The Real is the very unbearable locus trapped within these logics of transformation – from the Imaginary (politics) to the Symbolic (the political) – and within the relations of affiliation and non-affiliation with them. These affiliations and their inversions are themselves an initial deviation from these logics, a deviation that constitutes the affiliation in reality. The civic subject is already always constituted in the deviations of *the Real*. The "unimaginability" of *the Real* is an initial deviation of both affiliation and non-affiliation of the *polis* subject. Politics is the imaginary, narcissistic, and personal level of aggression, the translation of the structural violence of the symbolic-political, which is rendered herewith under the concept of *Abjectivation*.

7

In engaging with the conceptual-political, I focus less on the range of political characteristics of ideologies – from democracy to monarchy or totalitarianism – except for a brief mention of the different kinds of totalitarian regimes.

Moreover, in mapping the conceptual field, the conceptuality herewith also haunts itself in a way that ultimately disrupts it. All of this corresponds metaphysically to the field in question, which is itself located in incoherence (an incoherence linked to the historical evolving of the concept as a concept which explores its own conceptuality and in the process revokes and renews itself through an internal motion). Thus, the conceptuality taking shape here is philosophically ample, but only in relation to itself rather than to the external world (though we may further realize that this "self" is the category of subjectivity that encounters the resonance of the other within it, under ever-changing historical conditions).

I place particular emphasis on the dimensions of *abjectivation* in the conceptual field of *the political*, in the sense of *objectification, as an elaboration* of Julia Kristeva's concepts of *abjectness and abjection*.[10] Namely, not merely in the sense of negating someone (you are not X; you are null and void; you are uprooted from...) but in the most profound sense of his/her constitution and his/her characterization through this very act of negativation. Thus, through the same act, this kind of dialectics negates and simultaneously coerces, generating the subject as *abject*.

Perhaps it would be better to propose terms such as abjection or self-negativation, suggesting that the subject is a participant in the process of negativation and abjectivation within the political, and in the process, enters the political. However, I am more concerned here with the institutional dimension than with the existential or psychological constitution of the subject. Hence, I persevere with *negativation* and *abjectivation*.

Abjectivation expresses a profound action, beginning with the subject's initial constitution as "being" *abject*. The *abject* or the foreclosed is the subject-object of *abjection* and abjectivation. *Abjection* is the condition in which this *subjobject* exists, as elaborated following Kristeva and her treatment of the *ab* as a negating prefix.

8

The exercise of reducing *the political* to the dimension of *abjectivation is an opportunity to sharpen* the question whether the political is in its very foundation an act of abjectivation on all of its levels and not merely one of its characteristics, essential or foundational as it may be.

I treat *the political as the space deriving from the very concept of "political,"* that is, I understand the political as a space that reflects an *internal dynamic* within the conceptuality of the political, beginning with its Greek origins, but not limited to them, that is, in the dynamic played out in the so-called extra-conceptual reality, as a derivative of the concept of "the political" (following the Hegelian conception of reality trailing behind the concept's spirit, but not necessarily in full agreement with it).

Thus, *the political* is, at its core, a conceptual act enacted in the world. If it is possible to imagine an act devoid of conceptual context, this is not the case here. The political is not an act that embodies or expresses the *Being* free from any conceptual space, nor is it the concept in the sense of the political as expressing or being expressed within the internal space of subjectivity, for it experiences the political relations in the world prior to the birth of the concept or without it. If that were the case, we would be discussing *politics* as the space exercising (and activating) power relations between various subjects (including the State as subject). As if the word "politics" could exist under a depiction indifferent to its being a derivative of the conceptual world.

Once this is understood – if at all – I can proceed to the next, or perhaps the parallel, stage, where we consider the concept of *abjectivation* also as an expression of the political. For me, this word – as well as the *being* or the act it describes – cannot be but a derivative of the conceptuality of the political. All this while recognizing that both *abjectivation* and *the political* are phenomena which exist and develop within a conceptual space, and from there reality is constructed and not the other way around. Both are terms through which the essence of the word is materialized in the world.

In contrast to *abjectivation*, there is the phenomenon of *pre-political degradation* as an act that imagines itself free of the conceptual world of *the political, perhaps* even free of the conceptual space altogether. It seems to be an *affect* (imaginary, personal) of one body acting against another, as if the body could somehow exist as pre-political, as I attempt to do here, perhaps deliberately testing the limits of this possibility and failing to do so. *Abjectivation*, by contrast, refers to the way such an act is entangled in a much deeper exchange with the very conceptuality of the political and the symbolic order. *Abjectivation* is embedded in the internal organization of subjectivity, in that it is engaged with the political and with the very concept of the political, defining the relations between subjects, without writing off the understanding that this organization of subjectivity locates the subject at its most primary point, prior to becoming a political *thing* (*Ding*). Compare Lacan's comments[11] regarding the body before it becomes the subject of symbolic castration. But even at that earliest stage of non-affiliation, the subject is already a subject, for its existence is always *in relation to*. This is precisely what makes the subject the object of the political, as I argue with (and against) Aristotle: the subject is the principal object of the political and of the State (which, according to Hegel, is itself a developing conceptual universe that materializes through the regulation of material and subjective reality and the relation between them).

When I refer to the citizen in the Greek sense – *politēs* – I refer first and foremost to one who carries the load of a concept, a concept that is itself a sub-concept of the larger concept of the political. First, he/she is a citizen of the *Concept-State* of *the political*, and only secondarily a citizen of Israel or Guatemala. Hence, when we speak of the citizen *in the political, we refer to the citizen in* the concept of the political, and subsequently *in the State, a citizen* of Aristotle's word and the space of the concept. A citizen of the ink-line written on the pages of Aristotle's *Politics*.

9

> It is clear, then, that the city [*polis*] both exists by nature and is prior in nature to the individual. For if an individual is not self-sufficient when sep-arated, he will be in a similar state to that of the other parts in relation to the whole. And anyone who cannot live in a community with others, or who does not need to because of his self-sufficiency, is no part of a city, so that he is either a wild beast or a god.[12]

Aristotle's definition of the wild beast rests on the metaphysical assumption that the essence of a thing is determined by its end. If the telos of the human being is to thrive within the goodness of the state, then that is his nature. *The wild beast* is such because, being situated within this metaphysical articu-lation, it does not conform with the logic of ends that inscribes the essential and the natural retroactively. It is natural for the human being, from the vil-lage to the polis, to desire the communal, and since we operate by a logic that privileges the *whole* over the *partial*, the individual who does not belong to the collective is either a wild beast or a god (largely inferior or superior to the human being). *The metaphysical inscription of the human being as a citizen creates the citizen retroactively and dialectically* as a component deviating from that general rule.[13]

My insistence on this reading of the citizen stems from a close reading of the quote from Aristotle's *Politics*. His initial definition posits the human as a citizen of the *polis*, but in the very next breath, he implies a deviation. Perhaps, the text subverts itself in the sense that the immediate reservation enacts a kind of internal deconstruction of the initial claim it has just proposed as a thing whose feasibility is not definitive. As if there were two theses here, locked in an internal dialectical tension: on the one hand, the civil is born within Aristotle's concept of the political; on the other, Aristotle gives rise to the citizen condi-tionally, under the concept of negativity, as the one not non-affiliated with the polis.

If we read Aristotle against and with Aristotle (in the Lacanian sense of *Kant with* [*avec*] *Sade*),[14] it stands to reason that the citizen is rather that which is emitted from the concept of the political, someone either inferior or superior to the human being. For the less-than or more-than human, or less-than or more-than citizen, demonstrate first and foremost the deeply aporetic essence of the human being, who is never comfortably located, and forever more-than or less-than him/herself. Unlike the wild beast, which is one and the same with itself, the human is defined precisely by its impossibility to be defined. Also, this human – who deviates more or less from what is human and less or more from what is required for the political – is precisely what serves as raw material for the political. Incidentally, we may find here the logical equivalence between the conceptuality of the human and the conceptuality of the citizen: neither is ever in full conformity with itself, and both, by virtue of their identical deviation, are connected to the conceptual space of *the political*.

It should be noted that Aristotle does not refer to those who might be incidentally not affiliated with the state, but to those who are naturally so. Namely, such might be the human being: one who, by nature, does not belong to the state and yet resides in it, therefore assigned a degraded status, that of abjectivation. And who is this abject figure if not all of us, each and every one of us in our singular, jouissant nature? For we are originally born, hurled, in the Heideggerian sense of *Geworfenheit*, into the State and into the political, with our naked bodies. The desire and need for affiliation, as Aristotle presents them, are co-constructed with the body and with speech, albeit a remainder of jouissant resistance – in the Lacanian sense of *jouissance* – always persisting, meandering, it is a pre-subjective remainder, but also the product of being-the subject itself, an emanation from an ancient residue of one of the phases in the creation of the subject.

10

The concept of *the political* institutionalizes and regulates the relations between the subjects and between the subjects *and themselves*. It does so by reflecting the subjectivity of the subjects whose relations are subjected to their neighbors within the space of subject-relations. Moreover, the political generates subjectivity itself in its movement from its resisting corporeal dimension to the sense of companionship. Namely, subjectivity is born out of a primary discursive presupposition of the impossibility of assimilation. And this impossibility is already inscribed in the political, and therefore, so is the *abjectivation* of that subjectivity.

Within the conceptual space of *the political*, the relations between the various identified citizens of the *politēs* are manifested through a complex logic of the many agents directed by a two-way vector, reminiscent of Freud's concept of the *Überdeterminierung* (overdetermination) in *The Interpretation of Dreams* (1900) and its use in *For Marx* (1965) by Louis Althusser. Namely, the political is the chain of determination between countless subjects and their countless self-identities, in the sense previously mentioned, and between countless resistant and abjectivized kernels. A multiplicity of two-way relations. The political and its institutional extensions within the world of politics institutionalize the relations within this entire complex of multiple determination, so that each and every one of its components finds itself in simultaneous conversation with various innumerable others. The conversation includes each subject in its position of *abjectivation*, holding something of the primary founding kernel.

The political also administers the various formulas of:

- the vectors between the subjects and themselves,
- and the vectors within the different blocks of subjects, and between the blocks.

This is based on the assumption that every such block of subjects has a *mind* of a single subject. Namely, that each political block is like a *polis* with its own *politēs*, in an identical complex from the fractal point of view, for it operates according to a subject's logic (the fractal being a structure of natural replications of a superior hierarchical structure containing identical reproduced structures, such as the structure of a tree, its branches, sub-branches, and sub-sub-branches, etc., or the structure of the crystalline geometry of snowflakes). Each block administers its relations with its subjects according to the logic of multiple determination. The block itself, as political, has the same relations with the block above it, a relation aware of it being a block-subject in a relation with and toward the block above it.

But the logic of multiple determination also produces a noise that obscures the primary given: the foundational moment of the civic subject into a political block is a moment of abjectivation of that system, stemming from the subject's condition of not being affiliated. The subject is not cast into the world affiliated; it is cast into its being "non-affiliated." This is its affiliative identity in the structure that generated it. We will see how the relations of *abjectivation* between the subjects and themselves appease and regulate the anxiety of this affiliated non-affiliative.

The political also orchestrates the different formulas of the vectors between subjects, including the relations between the vectors and themselves, where the vectors constitute ideological frameworks purporting to characterize the relations between segments of the block and the State.

11

It is the political that facilitates the principal relation of the *complex of interactions subjects-vectors toward the supra-subject*, whether the supra-subject is a State, a king, a city, a municipality, a government, a party, or a president, namely formalizations of the subject. The political concept is what organizes the signification of these relations so that it may regulate the hostility inherent in the relations among the subjects themselves and between them and the supra-subject. This hostility is the result of their being cast into a conceptual space of relations; although this is subsequent to their entry into the familial or the lingual spaces, in the political, there is an exceptional conceptual regulation of the spirit's domination over subjects.

The organization of the political complex of relations between the subjects and themselves and between them and the supra-subject *polis* is consensual (a kind of strange fusion between conflict and consent), a permanent interior consent among the various agents, a consensual conflict marked by perpetual, constitutive *abjectivation* of the subjects and even of the relations or sub-relations between them. These relations are ideological; ideological positions become civic subjects, as do the other human beings within the complex, and so ideologies as citizens of the political are also situated in a perpetual liminal state of *abjectivation* and constitution. Ideologies are subjects in the sense that they become figures of desire and of its lack.

This implies the possibility to propose the same model of structurality regarding the relations of the political supra-subject with its "self" (as suggested above, that the self of the subjects reflects their position in relation to the others): here, the self of the supra-subject is characterized by its relations with itself as a self-intensifying, self-agitating agent. This may indeed be puzzling.

In question is the mode through which the concept of the political makes it possible for the supra-subject to experience itself as a dynamic of self-consensual conflict. Such is the situation when the governing space rests within an internal, eternal conflict with the bureaucratic space concerning questions of legitimacy and power.[15] It is an internal dynamic of multiple determinations within the various agents, identical to the one operating within the civic complex of the *polis*.

And if there are two levels of multiple determination:

• Between the field of subjects and themselves and between them and the supra-subject;
• Between the field of internal agents within the supra-subject and between the supra-subject and its officials;

then, it follows that the intra-governing picture within the supra-subject is like a fractal replica of the relation between the supra-subject and the subjects it serves. In any case, the supra-subject serves the citizen-subjects (with all the genealogical dynamics of the word "sub-ject," with its Greek and Latin antecedence, from subject to autonomous self)[16] by virtue of its relation to them as "supra," as well as by virtue of being itself a subject.

12

This system is significantly expressed in various forms of despotic regimes, whether right-wing or left-wing. It is evident, particularly in the case of the communist regime, where the supra-subject presents itself (and effectively operates accordingly) as acting in the "service" of its subjects who are subjected to its direct and absolute sovereignty: the sovereign provides for them the service of subservience to the conceptual space it had determined for them.

Evidently, this is not open to any kind of "bourgeois," "liberal" deliberation vis-à-vis the subjects (I point to this with some irony). The deliberation is carried out in their name and for their sake, as evidenced in the Soviet show trials. This form of "discussion" is possible in the case of communism because the subjects are being totally assimilated in the supra-subject itself, as being embodied in the very utopian fascination of the supra-subject with itself as the redeemer of all subjects, in the ecclesiastic sense of the *Corpus Christi*. Ask Dostoevsky, who heard it from the Grand Inquisitor.

In what concerns the fascist versions of totalitarianism, whether in the form of classical fascism, such as the Italian fascism or the German Nazism, or even pre-fascist populisms the like of Hungary, Israel, or Poland (forgive me the unskilled mix), there persists a shared conceptuality, where the supra-subject identifies with a very particular ethnic component in the citizenry of the *polis*, coloring the *polis* a unified ethnic color. In doing so, it writes off the conceptual basis of the *polis* as an idea, turning it into a reduced space of politics and in the process neutralizing *the political*. In these cases, the dynamic is at the same time more complicated and more simple: there emerges the possibility for a clearer distinction between the dimension of *abjectivation* and the moment of constitution of the "proper" ethnic subject, between two categories of citizens: the loyal (or more precisely, the non-disloyal to the ideology of the ethnos) and the disloyal (to the same ideology).

In leftist totalitarianism, there persists a fundamental intricacy that precludes the possibility of a decent, stable citizenship: in the case of fascist or nationalist-populist regimes as well, both citizens and non-citizens are always under the threat of *abjectivation* and of the permanent "positive" (re)constitution of their status. In the Soviet totalitarian model, however, there exists an initial universal mix applicable to all without exception: everyone is under the threat of the guillotine, including Robespierre and Stalin (at least potentially). It appears then that fascism emerges initially from a subtle dimension of the ethnos, while leftist totalitarianism installs from the outset a universal guillotine of abjectivation for everyone.

13

By its very nature, the supra-subject[17] is representative of the citizens-subjects, whereby they are subjected to the concept imagined in its own mind. This is where a series of the subjects' *abjectivation* by the supra-subject begins. The *abjectivation* of *servitization*. Servitization is the will of the supra-subject that shapes the will of its subordinated subjects to conform to the formulas, "I serve you" and "please comply."[18]

A certain propagandistic rhetoric may be detected here, but if we remain with it, we overlook the dimension of the *abjectivation* of the subject from the ideological standpoint of the supra-subject, who, as an (imagined) persona, truly believes in it.

Liberation from subjection to this formula can only exist following a momentary, formulaic invention (asymptotically approaching zero) that prevents fixing relations of servitude on any side. For example, the concept of servitude can cunningly be reversed to each fragment within the fractal map or within the map of multiple determination, or alternatively, enter into exchange formulas: service in exchange for service.

An additional condition is recognizing the function of the hostile sense of *abjectivation* as a unifying adhesive. It is a form of cohesion, but always a tardy one, a reactionary nostalgic perspective regarding a lost ethno-political-economic space. This tardiness reproduces the self-inscription of the subject over and over again under the dialectic of *abjectivation* and legitimation, under the play of the non-not-citizen and the non-not-non-citizen.

14

The organization of the community and its boundaries most often occur through negation. One is not accepted into the community on the basis of being "A," but rather on the basis of being "not-not-A." Not because one is Jewish, but because one is "not-not-Jewish,"[19] following Aristotelian (non-) logic: you are a citizen not because you are a political animal, but because you are not-not-political.

Perhaps this example is a demagogic maneuver due to its obvious historical background. Moreover, the concept of "Jewishness" is always characterized primarily by its conceptuality. Namely, the conceptual essence of it, or the reference of its conceptuality is its being a concept, and what is this concept if not the tension of a *negative tautology*, not in the sense that "a Jew is one who is a Jew," but rather "a Jew is one who is not-not a non-Jew"; the Jew is primarily one who is not a Gentile.

And if we move away from the political of the State to the political of the couple, then you are my wife not because you are my wife, but because you are not-not my wife; you are my wife precisely because you are not married to someone else. The primary tautology of "you are my wife because you are my wife" is possible in a space that is non-institutional and not subject to a rabbinical or civil contract. But then again, does the concept "my wife" lose its significance? Not necessarily, because the concept itself is already an institution, regardless of any contractual subjection to a particular institution.

A concept is always already an institution, or perhaps an institution unto itself, in need of deviating from itself through physical, mental, cultural, and bureaucratic structures. The negative tautology, however, lies at the foundation of the institutional pact designed to preserve the double negation. This shows that the institution exists already within the concepts of State, king, and *polis*, and everything else is merely temporary and regional envelopes.

15

Worth emphasizing is that the quote from Aristotle refers to the "natural" aspect of the choice to be a citizen or not or being selected for citizenship or not. This concerns the term *phusis* (from "to appear," "to grow," and also "law of nature"), whose precise significance in the sense the Hebrew understands it today is not very clear. The intended significance seems to indicate a *Being* developing naturally, as is the case with animals and plants, as opposed to *tékhnē* (art or craft), which denotes an existence fostered by an external agent and is part of the conceptual space of the *nómos* (law), distinguished from *phusis*.[20] The civic dimension (and its negation) stems from phenomena inherently; it is not an aleatory one but lies in their most fundamental element.

This dimension of civic essentiality allows for the *polarity* of negation and double negation of that being. Consequently, it also enables the danger expected from the State. The double negation facilitates the political capture of the subject through the oscillation between the two negations – the negation of negation and the negation of affirmation – producing articulations for the community boundaries as well as the organization of the articulations within the community.

16

But the social space nonetheless manages to organize itself without overtly visible signs of negations or of the negation of negations. This is also true for the dimensions of fusion and delay, for the fusion always occurs through the logic of delay and retrospectively, *retro-fusion*, as it were. Both reward us within the residual social, ever-changing relations but nevertheless maintained under the logic of symbolic structurality, and within the representational space that still preserves the relations between the symbol and the symbolized (as imaginary as they may be).

The fusion sustains in the Lacanian sense of *the quilting point* (*point de capiton*), retroactively justifying the negation and in this way stabilizing the political structure.[21] Only a momentary disengagement, which is practically (nearly) impossible, could enable a political space that rewards citizens without subjecting them to a veiled, permanent threat of negation and the negation of negation.

That said, no complete alternative for *abjectivating* politics is offered herewith. Perhaps, only a *continuous* deconstruction of the relations within the subject-complex named "the State" can preserve a certain degree of good for the citizen. For deconstruction, albeit a possible negative allusion, is a nonviolent one, in that it deconstructs only the discursive space, without harming the body of the subject of the discourse, as opposed to the State, whose violence is exerted upon the body or the subject. When the State assaults the discourse, it will ultimately inevitably assault the subject-body.

Moreover, it seems that the regulation of hostility and its designation as pathology overlook the fact that these are also the *prosthesis* sustaining this entire metaphysical structure, generated through the very emergence of the Greek word *politikos*, with all its Athenian conceptual, cultural, and metaphysical charge (including the retroactive inscription of past periods of time predating the concept, as well as from its geographical political-spatial perspective).

17

Who then is the object of that political hostility, notably today, when it seems that human progress has done so little to reduce the clarity of the other's anxiety? Signifying the other as *abject*, reinternalizing it only to disgorge it as *abjectivation*, is a significant prosthetic moment in the politics of hostility today, possibly in every dimension of the political, insofar as it is always hostile to something that is *not affiliated with or to the subject for the subject*. Namely, the political within the subject (any subject whatsoever) of *abjectivation* emerges as the political under the lack within the subject primarily in relation to him/herself as subject, and only secondarily in relation to the other, supra-subject.

The *other* exploits this dynamic for its own benefits, not always successfully, while the suffering subject rarely knows how to work with this raw material of hostility, unless it projects it onto another subject within the community or onto the community at large or the political supra-community. What takes shape here is a triangular dynamic, articulated through the prepositions: in-the subject, of-the subject, and for-the subject. Namely, there emerge several relational possibilities regarding the dimension of *abjectivation* for the subject, and perhaps even the possibility of the fixation of *the* subject (lacking movement). Accordingly, there are various ways for the subject to experience the political abjection within it – of content, of affiliation, of contribution on its behalf, or even as its definition as such. From these formulations, it is evident that the abject within the subject is not structurally fixed in any one configuration but is rather dynamic. It may be formulated as follows: the subject's existence as abject is its conceptuality along the axis of time (and not its realness), or its movement along the axis of time; for example, from present to past or from past to future. It is in perpetual motion, and the political other is in its pursuit, seeking to catch up with it and signify it according to its own needs.

18

What is *abjectivation*? It is *my* conceptual understanding following Kristeva's notion of *abjection*, regarding the particular founding of the *Other* subject under the status of the *abject* during its birth in reversal as an object of *my* subjectivity. Namely, an object within the canal of my subjectivity. The Other is a subject which becomes a repelled object through abjectivation, not in a neutral place but within the very canal of my subjectivity. Introducing the *Other* into me, into my body, and into my intestines, via the anus or the mouth, and then vomiting or defecating it. Let it pass through the repelled track of my body and my subjectivity and its desire to imagine itself without a smeared canal. Initially, the abjected other, in its foundational state of abjectivation, which precedes abjection in a *totally imagined* antecedence, is situated in its absolute separateness as an *Other-subject*, preceding its *Geworfenheit* and oriented toward my presence. Namely, before its presence vis-à-vis me as subject within the field of the State's subjects.

The concept of the political has brought the Other to exist as a balloon, launched from the universe outward, but on its way out, before its loathsome expulsion, it became momentarily (almost not at all) anatomically internal, in a real sense. But this is an empty moment, not even imaginable. Through this movement, the abjectivated enters the political through a deficient time close to zero, and is scornfully cast out.

The purpose of this complicated description is an attempt to elucidate the fact that the inward and outward movement of abjectifying is so rapid and brief that it seems not to occur at all. As if it were an external expulsion that has not passed through an inward-outward motion. An expelled being that has not passed through the motion of expulsion. A citizen not having passed through the motion of becoming a citizen. A prisoner skipping over the motion of being denied. A racialized entity without having gone through the motion of racialization.

In the discourse of racism, this is most transparent, but also in the discourse of the political, the subject is constantly perceived under *abjectivation*, suspected of non-affiliation, which requires exerting discursive, ideological, or even physical power over it, that is, over the imagined body representing it. Then, the imagined body of the State controls the imagined body supposed as belonging to the subject. When it is identified in terms of a body, incarcerated, held in a room, or physically or domestically restricted under lockdown, the elusive subject is in a position convenient for the State.

Political abjectivation is an act that constitutes the object's objecthood, down to the root of its subjectivity, without the subject being aware of being swallowed and immediately expelled. *Abjectivation* is a political practice toward the subject as the *Other* of the political practice. This practice is performed by the State-subject, which perceives this extimate otherness as inherently inaccessible, as apparently evident. For the supra-subject, this otherness is extimate because it is simultaneously external and internal to the State, an inherent internal subject but at the same time excessive. This excess of jouissance is always maintained as a reserve for a critical moment; the moment of the political act.

19

In the political act, the extimate subject will know how to extract from itself its singular excess, albeit an excess of an internal lack rather than an exterior protrusion. The subject in belatedness is always too late in changing its timing. The possibility for change will come from an unexpected otherness, when the subject knows how to rise above itself in a way that its entire subjectivity is channeled and expressed revolutionarily in its very excess. In this singular moment, the considerations concerning the cost of the act and the fear of the act do not vanish; they are not repressed nor reinterpreted through the supra-subject's perspective on the ego, for the fear is linked to a strange identification with the state's mechanism of intimidation. Something new will emerge: through its own singular excess, the ego will know how to look straight in the eyes of the supra-subject and the Law and inform them that the validity of the law is no longer valid, namely that the Law remains law, but in suspension: in the suspension of fear. This may only occur if, in that fatal moment, the ego links its excess to the space of another ego's excess: the space of love, the space of community, the community of excess, or the moment of the birth (of the consciousness) of a community.[22]

Yet, the entire dimension of excess cannot escape the fact that the political is the game of relations among separated subjects under a single Big Subject that preserves their separateness in order to preclude various formations of resisting blocks. In other words, even the very singular excess is a product of the sovereign (which, as previously noted, is itself caught within a dynamic of infinite consensual conflict between the supra-subject forces within it). It is not possible to escape from this ironic dialectic, for the very concept of the political is constructed a priori through the crafting of the subject's abjectivation, the crafting of the subject's birth, and the recurring process of swallowing and expelling; the singularity of the ego is constituted through the very domination of the political over the subject.

20

The political concept, within which the supra-subject resides, establishes various compounds of separated blocks and separated subjects with diverse and peculiar coalitions, so that amid the turmoil of consensual conflict, one thing is preserved: the subjugation of the abjectivation-subject to the system. Several main phases are manifested here for the civic subject:

• The abjectivation of the subject as non-affiliated.
• The preservation of its singular excess.
• The preservation of the subject's bondage to the space of the *polis*.

The political is constantly sullied by abjectionality, so that it may regulate its relations with internal subjects that do not serve the supra-subject or with external subjects threatening the contractual relations between the supra-subject and its subordinate subjects.

This mixture between the political, which is the field of mixing and connecting, and abjection, which is the field of separating or non-connective connecting, is but a harmony between two essences artificially separated by two concepts whose conceptuality generates two essences, in the sense that a concept wounds the universe with a new space of existence as a result of a concept (i.e., the concept injects into the universe a bubble of existence, which prompts the encounter of the real with the concept's translation into raw actuality). The two concepts within the ideational space fantasize for us two interacting planes, although they are one and the same essence. How to bridge between two utterly different essences, a relation of contract and decency, and one of abjectivation and hostility, akin to two parallel universes that are also of the same existence?

A difficulty is revealed here in the understanding of the relations between three components: (1) the universe of the political, (2) the universe of abjection, and (3) the universe of the political-abjection sameness. An example of the processes of abjectivation and love in the political sphere may elucidate the mixing of relations between the excesses of abjectivation and the regulating of the political: in the contemporary case of Israel, (Prime Minister Netanyahu and his government), all the different segments of Israeli society have been submerged in the government's schemes for over a decade without the possibility to escape, witnessing the collapse of the democratic political project into a space that is singularly political in the most self-serving, narrow, reductive sense, devoid of the conceptual crutch, as it were.

21

We might ask in what way *abjection*, as a concept within the philosophical space organizing the political, but also as a subject-constituting entity of the political subjects within the Israeli space, constitutes the political space in contemporary Israel.

I attempt to answer this question from a bird's-eye view, observing from above the occurrences within that field. This vantage point is not necessarily indifferent, for the bird covets certain signifiers within the field and also desires to land in it and gather fragments of signifiers to build its nest. Moreover, a certain suspension from geography occurs momentarily, in the sense of the inscription of the earth. The movement that the bird identifies in the space of Israeli-ness is one of both self-abjection politics and the abjectivation of the other.

In the first place, various factors within the communal space are engaged in intra-communal abjectivation, namely, in signifying themselves as traumatic for being a part of the State–subjects complex, as a mythical-historical inscription of a structural and conceptual reality. The entire inscription or history of their identity rests upon an abject condition, such as the trauma of victimhood. The victimhood does not halt at this point but passes through the dimension of abjectivation as a superfluous or abominable object that must be expelled or excluded. This is the object of the self-victimizing subject, which, under the mythology of self-victimhood, produces an easily operable abjectivation of other subjects within the State. To some extent, all communities are engaged in this, ranging from those perceived as hegemonic to the most marginalized.

Love in the political is not even the other side of the coin of abjectivation and hostility. It is that same affective space of *hostilove*, in which the libidinal both likes and hates various subjects within the space and places them under different positions according to the fractal relation between the subjects and the supra-subject, and within the supra-subject, between the bureaucratic subjects and the supra-subject. This adds up to a space that **activates its** various subjects through its watchful eye and charges them with an excess of preferential treatment or systemic neglect. In question is not an ambivalence of hatred and love but a strong will vis-à-vis the civic positioning within the political space.

Ultimately, we must steer clear of the danger of conceptually separating hatred from love, of separating hostility and abjectivation from the effect of attachment. Otherwise, love is grafted within the concept of the political woven as a State, toward a leader through a particular group, while another group casts upon that leader tremendous hostility. Then "just not Bibi" and "only Bibi" become the reductions of the conceptual mechanisms of abjectivation and attachment, and do not allow the development of a state whose orientation is mixing the subjects within it, an orientation that is already complex, for the State also needs to run around on their behalf within an impossible framework of multiple determination. Any such personal reduction enables the State to cover up and continue to conceal the fundamental question of our being cast into it, of its being a Leviathan engaged in swimming while devouring juicy planktons, each with its unique flavor.

Notes

1 Aristotle, *Aristotle's Politica*, ed. W. D. Ross, Clarendon Press: Oxford, 1957.
2 Aristotle, *Politics*, transl. C.D.C. Reeve, Indianapolis: Hackett, 1998.
3 My compulsive preoccupation here with the signifiers of *Abjectivation* and the political derives from a growing sense – intensified by the current powerful protests against Prime Minister Netanyahu's government – that the political space in Israel is saturated with acts of abjectivation and negativation performed by the state toward its citizens, by citizens against the State, by citizens against each other, by citizens against non-citizens, by non-citizens against citizens, by non-citizens against the State, and by non-citizens against each other (e.g., conflicts between the various Palestinian movements).
4 Sigmund Freud, "Negation", in *The Standard Edition of the Complete Psychological Works of Sigmund Freud, vol. 19: The Ego and the Id and Other Works*, transl. James Strachey, London: Hogarth Press, 1961, pp. 235–239, 1925.

5 Carl Schmitt, *The Concept of the Political*, transl. George D. Schwab, Chicago: University of Chicago Press, 1996.
6 Adi Ofir, "Between the Sanctification of Life and Its Abandonment: In Place of an Introduction to Homo Sacer", in *Technologies of Justice: Law, Science, and Society* [in Hebrew], ed. S. Lavi Tel Aviv: Ramot Publishing, pp. 353–394, 2003.
7 Chantal Mouffe, *On the Political*, New York: Routledge, 2005.
8 Jean-Luc Nancy, *Chroniques Philosophiques*, Paris: Éditions Galilée, 2004.
9 https://tinyurl.com/66tnhyjb.
10 Julia Kristeva, *Powers of Horror: An Essay on Abjection*, transl. Leon S. Roudiez, New York: Columbia University Press, 1982.
11 Jacques Lacan, *The Seminar, Book VII - The Ethics of Psychoanalysis, 1959–1960*, ed. Jacques-Alain Miller, transl. Dennis Porter, New York: W.W. Norton & Co., 1992.
12 Aristotle, *Politics*, transl C.D.C. Reeve, Indianapolis: Hackett, 1998.
13 [Translator's note: The author uses the word "klal" which in Hebrew refers both to "rule" (as noun) as well as to "totality, whole, public"].
14 Jacques Lacan, "Kant avec Sade", *Écrits*, Paris: Seuil, 1966.
15 Michel Foucault, *Power/Knowledge: Selected Interviews and Other Writings 1972–1977*, transl. C. Gordon et al., ed. C. Gordon, Brighton: Harvester, 1980.
16 Etienne Balibar, "Citoyen sujet", *Cahiers Confrontation*, no. 20 (Hiver 1989):23–48.
17 See also Louis Althusser, "Ideology and Ideological State Apparatuses (Notes towards an Investigation)", in *Lenin and Philosophy and Other Essays*, transl. Ben Brewster, London: New Left Books, pp. 127–186, 1971.
18 Jean-Jacques Rousseau, *The Social Contract*, transl. Maurice Cranston, London: Penguin Books, 1968.
19 Cf. Slavoj Žižek, "Neighbors and Other Monsters: A Plea for Ethical Violence," in *The Neighbor: Three Inquiries in Political Theology*, ed. Slavoj Žižek, Eric L. Santner, and Kenneth Reinhard, Chicago: University of Chicago Press, 2006.
20 Aristotle, *Metaphysics*, transl. Hugh Tredennick, Cambridge, MA: Harvard University Press, 1961.
21 Jacques Lacan, *The Seminar, Book III - The Psychoses*, ed. Jacques-Alain Miller, trans. Russell Grigg, New York: W.W. Norton & Co., 1993.
22 There is a Žižekian aroma to this formulation. See especially Slavoj Žižek, *The Puppet and the Dwarf: The Perverse Core of Christianity*, Cambridge, MA: MIT Press, 2003.

Chapter 3

Civil Anxiety
The Tent Protest and the Theo-Political Uncanniness

Judah has gone into exile
Because of misery and harsh oppression;
When she settled among the nations,
She found no rest
>   Lamentations 1: 3, in response to the destruction of the First Temple

[…] Structuralism or not, it seems to me that nowhere is the negation of the subject the issue […] I do not consider it legitimate in any way to write that the structures do not descend to the street, for if there is anything that the May events have demonstrated, it is precisely the descent of the structures to the street. The fact that the events are written in the same place that this descent occurred is simply proof of what is very often, and even most often, interior to what we call the act, that which it does not recognize in itself.[1]

In what follows, I intend to address an acute, essential symptom of the Israeli discontent in its economic, religious, and cultural domains, which surfaced during the Tent Protest in the summer of 2011, notably during the events that occurred around the encampment set up along Rothschild Boulevard in Tel Aviv. Based on Jacque Lacan's theoretical tenets, I contend that the civil and the theological, which constitute each other, consciously deny or repress the presence of their self-constitution in their other, even if it is not in the same fashion or to the same degree of radicalism. Namely, the oppressing, insufferable Real of each one of them is equivalent to the very emergence of repression of the fact that the act of the subject's constitution is via the other and not by the subject alone.

I shall refer here, mainly, to the mainstream of the protest and, more specifically, to the image of the protesters as children of the *crème de la crème* of Israel, the *privileged Ashkenazi* middle class as "Cottage cheese children."[2]

I argue that this is (supposedly) *merely* an exterior image that constituted their being, which establishes the basis for the subject inscribed herein = the community of protestors belonging to the Ashkenazi social class as part of its

DOI: 10.4324/9781003667339-3

habitus. In this respect, scrutinizing the stereotypical register of the "Ashkenazi" permits us to examine the phantasm of the Israeli who wishes to be "Ashkenazi" (in the sense of becoming) trapped in the Ashkenazi habitus (liberal, secular, leftist, cultured, Zionist, and so forth).

Most protestors aimed to act under the civil agenda to reduce the general and the personal Israeli anxiety, the anxiety of the civil experience in Israel. On the level of representation, we may interpret the protest, as it has been occasionally presented externally, as an attempt to rebuff this anxiety, this discontent, by isolating the civil subject (in three aspects, which are equal from the phantasmatic perspective): the subject, the civil, and the civil subject), undressing its wrap of anxiety. I would like to dwell upon what is perceived as "merely" an exterior image, and consequentially, on the expelled or burdening Other of the civil discourse, as embodied in the protest. I have chosen to define this Other as "theological" (a dimension much more comprehensive than the religious aspects of the political); it comprises two main axes of the wide theo-political: the local-national and the structural-universal.

To sharpen the discussion of the effacement or the repression of the theological in the civil arena of the Tent Protest, I shall address the mediating motifs (not without complication) between the civil-secular dimension and the various dimensions of the theo-political, and particularly to the local archetype of home – as surfaced during different central occasions in the protest. I will discuss the unhomely *(Unheimlich)* aspect of this archetype in connection with Freud's discussion of the *Unheimlich* anxiety - the *Angst* - which is the experience of the subject's encounter with *the Real*. Following Freud's and Lacan's psychoanalytical thought, I will present an outline for discussing the discontent related to Israeli subjectivity, ostensibly under the image of the "Ashkenazi," a discontent pertaining strictly to the constitution of the subject, the constitution of his/her theo-political, constitution within a radical other - real and distressing. I name this element the "**Supra-homely**."

***

This essay opens with a resonant between an ancient biblical citation and a modern French psychoanalytical one; both contain lamentations on subjects distant from one another but similar in their encounter with the revolutionary or eschatological trauma of the event (not in the sense of individual subjects but of the subjects of the community of protestors that constitutes the individual subject, the subject towards-eschatology).

This discussion, which seeks to learn about the subjectivity of the protest, whose description of experience may echo those subjective situations, does not bear a sociological or merely a sociological nature, namely, it does not affiliate itself with such academic-research disciplines but explores the possibility of a psycho-sociology.

Merely civil. In the following superfluous words, I shall attempt to present a few points of view - that may or may not complete each other, that could unite into one surprising, vanishing point – related to the rebellious event that took place in Israel in the summer of 2011 and was named the "Tent Protest." The following point is particularly astonishing due to its seeming exteriority to the social eventuation. It seems that the event in question exposed itself as a surprising event in itself, both in relation to its eruption and to its forceful continuation, thus to some extent positioning itself as exterior to what the obvious flux of public life and its (anti-civilian?) contents, as if it sparked from an unconscious seed, therefore seemingly out of nothing (from the public's phantasmatic point of view).

Reflecting on the preceding decades, quite a few hints were scattered that could allude to the coming events. But the civil outbreak of this accumulation took everyone by surprise in its consolidation to a mass-being that surpassed each of its participants, including those who started the big fire thinking they were merely amusing themselves by lighting a few matches of protest. Moreover, under what adjective are we to understand this historic episode when its various components sought to tie themselves merely to civil life and set the occurrence in motion under the civil, and merely civil, agenda?

Again, perhaps the key lies in the confining "merely," perhaps in the foreclosed or apathized other/s of the civil. Furthermore, this inquest poses a dilemma vis-à-vis this "may" as well, a dilemma that stems from my fear (and a source of encouragement as well) of encountering the expected argument that the following is *unfounded*, an idea whose defense, somewhat ironically, dialectically reinforces my central thesis. I seek to expose the footprints of the apathized irrelevancy of the civil discourse, for which this irrelevancy is taken for granted, the discourse that emphasizes its presence through its absence and which is indeed linked to what I term "the theological."

Considering the slogans spread around the protest and the various newspaper columns written during this social upheaval that referred to the inurement of "the civil society," we may safely assume that among many of the protesting citizens, *understanding the social* is at times entrapped in a fantasy regarding the *civil kernel of the social*. The fantasy may perceive the general-civil as sub-conscious free and devoid of surplus, whether religious or not (and if it is a religious surplus, whether it is a religious group or not), as a dimension in which the citizens partake in a political act while weakening the authoritarian dimension at the basis of the political-hierarchical enforced on them. Namely, constitutionally, *the civil* is perceived as the ethical basis of *the social* and as actuating to break free from the other ideological dimensions as their other, a primary factor, raw in its foremost-material way (perhaps in the Marxist sense of the essential needs that precede ideology).

In this respect, *the civil* is a concept that sustains the democratic-horizontal phantasm from within which it situates itself in different historical moments against, within, outside, and alongside the phantasmatic axis termed in this article *the theological*, which is the paradigm of the vertical situation, any vertical position, even if it seems at times "merely" economic, philosophical, or juridical, and whether the problem is a local or a general-structural one.

Moreover, as we shall see, the horizontal and the vertical are not merely crucified onto each other, nor simply opposed to one another, as presented below. In this context, it is worth noting that the use of the term "theological" to indicate the *sub-social* or the *sub-civil* emerged as a response to the customary, commonsensical supposition (with or without relation to various current political philosophy discussions) that the civil basis of *the social* is free of surpluses. Albeit from a Marxist point of view, these surpluses should be termed as super-ideologies, for our purposes, and perhaps following Max Weber's discussion of the Protestant ethic behind and under the capitalistic evolution,[3] these are sub or un-conscious or obfuscated-denied surpluses.

I wish to note that we shall also open a discussion following the Marxist approach and define the lower limit, which is still pre-ideological (and pre-theological-submissive?), as related to the *homely-intimate* that seeks to be – at least in its fantasy – free of external ideological conditions (the vast gender implications of this topic warrant a separate discussion; moreover, I believe that gender power relations apply themselves to the homely pre-ideological, at least as it is naïvely situated in its imagined self-perspective). The civil perceives itself as persistent in its homely-intimate trend, extending it to an all-civilian intimacy (this accruement may develop in oppositional directions of either universal solidarity or national-exclusionary, the-ideo-logical one).

For me, *the theological* is related to the existential field in which the subject operates within relations of subjugation and submissiveness (or perhaps submissive love?) to the other or to a high-transcendent principle which is also *the social* per se. At the same time, *the religious and religion* are conspicuous paradigmatic incidents in which the manifestation of this submissiveness is coherent and exposed. The civil is the fantasy of breaking free from the same theological, which by *imagining itself as such*, already succeeds to break free (for the arena is internal-mental). However, that very *civil*, for instance under the perception of a social-civil contract, can produce a kind of general accruement in which the theological-transcendent resurfaces, surpassing itself, particularly in moments of communal rebellion and ecstasy demanding *justice*, when the mystical constitution of the birth of a community is rekindled,[4] demonstrating Durkheim's principle regarding the vital link between the religious experience and the communal one.[5]

The two subjects. In his examination of the concept of the modern citizen, Étienne Balibar confronts it with the concept of the subject.[6] The latter includes an intricate, internally contradictory, double entendre: the interior similarity between *subject* - both as a syntactic subject as well as an autonomous factor – and the previous layer in the political context of the *subjectus*, of the *sub*, which is the double concealed behind the civil veil, the king's subject, the subject of the general transcendent which is transcendent to himself, and now of the state's, the people's, and hence, the people's as a subject of the people and his own social contract, on the way to becoming a liberated non-civilian subject but a subject of the discourse of liberation. As Jean-Jacques Rousseau asserted in his *Social Contract*: "Whoever refuses to obey the general will shall be constrained to do so by the entire body; which means only that he will be forced to be free (I, vii, 8)."[7]

This tension also preoccupied Lacan when he underscored that the subject as the subject of the subconscious is the subject of the discourse of the (big) Other,[8] of the treasure of signifiers (and to some extent also the object of the object, such as manifested in the field of the gaze, the scopic field).[9] This concept of the subject is the opposite of the conscious ego. However, for Lacan, there is the unconscious/subject versus the conscious one, on the one hand, the unconscious being transcendent to the conscious one, and on the other hand, there is the subject who is transcended by the Other. These two types of otherness will be discussed as two levels of repression between the civil and the theological.

Repression or Denial or Indifference. These conceptual tensions at the basis of the civil vis-à-vis the theological, lead us to reflect on a surprising social phenomenon which aims at a new order, but in effect – and not surprisingly – is driven, among other things, by indifference or denial or almost total repression regarding its *other* aspects. When a latent negation establishes the self-definition of the very phenomenon, we might assume the existence of cultural repression or denial. In this context, we understand repression as an act directed at a component of the system that is concealed from consciousness at large (whether it is personal or collective), and this conscious part of this consciousness is ignorant of such component. Denial, as conscious resistance to something that is on the surface, is understood as an act reacting to such element which the consciousness perceives and lives by its surroundings yet ignores it as if it were not there.[10]

In our context, denial can be understood as **conscious** resistance to otherness, a refusal of it. In contrast, repression may be understood as **unconscious** resistance to the fact of denial itself, a sort of denial of the denial which therefore becomes unconscious (and as a result of which instigates the constitution of the subject based on the other-internal nucleus even more). Hence, secular repression removes the conscious fact of denying the dimension of its theological otherness. The encounter with this dimension of repression produces the anxiety of the real, followed by the rebellious act of removal (rebellious, though not revolutionary. As Lacan understood the student protests of 1968, this is not really about the removal of the Master but rather a different kind of removal, removal as denial).

In what follows, we shall ask precisely which mechanism is at play here. Whether it is repression or denial because the mechanism relating to the other of the phenomenon in question is one of negation, we wish to reformulate the massive protest organized by the young in Israel in the summer of 2011 according to the following assumption:

The sub-conscious of the *civil* is the *theological*, and the subconscious of the *theological* is the *civil*. They dwell in each other's residences, are secretly addressed to each other, deny or repress each other's presence, even if not in the exact same manner or to the same extent (in this context, the question arises whether we should dive into the Lacanian structural interior and exterior relations, or into relations of depth versus surface in the Jungian-Gnostic sense. Is this an unconscious pertaining to a bilateral refusal between the *theologic* and the *civil*, when the transcendent signifies a distant beyond, or is this a deep subconscious, the transcendent indicating truth versus the superficial?) Our claim echoes Lacan's:

> In the unconscious, which is not so much profound as it is inaccessible to conscious scrutiny, *it speaks*; the notion of a subject within the subject, transcending the subject has raised questions for philosophers since Freud first wrote *The Interpretation of Dreams*.[11]

We can add that if in relation to the *id* [in French, *ça* – which is also *this, it*] we refer to subject2 within subject1, then the opposite is also true, namely, the interior *id* –subject2 is a **subject as well**, with an unconscious of its own that is not necessarily deeper, but *extimate* to it; and the subject unconscious to it is precisely the conscious subject1.

This understanding may paint another picture in which the unconscious and the conscious are equally a specific consciousness, two interrelated specifics. While the latent unconscious lives in hiding, it is still unaware of the depth of its concealed life, repressing its very latent existence in the psyche of its exterior conscious, thus causing the existence of the conscious to be hidden and repressed by it. The unconscious is unaware of its being the first to be repressed; it refuses to accept this fact and denies it; if it has any regard for the conscious, any window of understanding towards the conscious, it will refuse to accept it as something independent of or separate from it. And what is the Real? Is it that which cannot be contained, the sheer existence of the other side that constitutes one subject or another?

The "empty wagon" and the dwarf. The question arising from the above is the following one: is the civil the unconscious of the deep-theological, one that the theological imagines as not deep, superficially conscious, and even as void, both in height as well as depth, a bilateral void? A void that fills up the empty wagon of the secular and is oblivious of the traditionalism existing in between, as if only two alternatives were possible, alternatives that leave nothing but a substantially automatic existence nothing short of inhuman.

But these two polar positions dwell in the ideological sphere, while the polarity itself (on the conscious level) is in its whole the outcome of the two distinct discourses: the theological one that invents in its opposite the discourse of the civil, the secular, and the heretic, and the secular one that is self-generated as such, as a subversion of the theological. Is the theological in Israel, which is forever on the doorstep of the civil, positioned as the repressed, or rather the denied, as *The* evident that has long became too transparent, or too ominous to be mentioned in the context of the sheer civil?

The civil and the theological. An initial clarification is warranted here: what are the theological and the civil, and what is the apocalyptic end at which they meet, almost against their will? First, we must underscore that while both the psychoanalytical and the philosophical concepts hold the structural walls of the original discourses that endowed them with their signifiers, they receive here re-inclusion, re-naturalization, perhaps in a colonialist manner, in which their sole significance stems from the present context, in that their present application – and not their mere definition – endows them with their present signified.

In this context, it seems that the significance of what has been termed here *the theological* refers to a concept related to the axis that vertically mediates between the human and its own realness (be it natural, political, and so forth) creating a wedge between them that mediates, obstructs, rectifies, regulates (the concepts of the divine, the religious, and the sanctified do not suffice here, because we are within a comprehensive discursive domain that only the concept of the *theological* is broad enough to contain; the spiritual and the religiously-experienced are not denied hereby but constructed through the prism of the theological discourse). As for the concept of the civil – it seems to refer to the domain that mediates horizontally, in a mediocre-intermediary way, and not supreme-transcendent (like the theological) between the human being and his/her realness within the confines of the state, so that the civilians approach each other through it without any vertical dimension directed at them (so that any vertical transcendent is continually being reduced towards the horizontal). The apocalyptic is a radical component within the theological. The tension between the horizontal and the vertical is most pertinent to our discussion of the Tent Protest, as evidenced by the term "representation" in the Hebrew publication of the protest's index, *Kriat Hamekha'a* [*The Voice of Protest*]:

> The identification of the economic system as a pyramid in which only a few enjoy the wealth and most of the population has no representation at the centers of power, has motivated many of the protests during 2011 [both in Israel and abroad, I.B.]) to constitute politically shallow or horizontal (as opposed to vertical) mechanisms (as opposed to the pyramid image).[12]

On the one hand, the theological, critically deconstructed, is momentarily successful in being neutralized from the apocalyptic radicalism, becoming moral, normative, appeased and liberal. On the other hand, the apocalyptic purifies the theological to a condensed form of it, perhaps only in which does the theological ultimately annuls itself exposing its civil kernel, thus insuring its self-annulment (in the sense of Hegel's *Aufhenbung) for itself*.

It seems that these days of tension and attraction-repulsion towards the apocalyptic vision of the war of the Jews against the rising Persian Empire reinforce the impression that the theological dimension and its radical end both agitate and restrain the civil discourses in Israel. This may also respond to the query whether we have wrongly reduced here the social and economic tensions to the secular/religious domain only. But if we have, it is a justified reduction, at least in relation to the Israeli/Zionist reality that has been moving from imagining it past under the Holocaust apocalypse towards a future nuclear apocalypse. Within this context, it is not unreasonable to argue that the very position that supports a dialectic complex relationship between the *civil* and the *theological*, as well as this kind of reduction, is more prevalent in the theological category, while in the civil one, prevails the very denial of this relationship. Moreover, it is possible to argue more categorically that the denial of the relationship between the *theological* and the *civil*, or the indifference to it, is the pronounced civil position. This is where the *civil* is born (in the self-denial from the theological point of view, and in cognitional independence from the civil point of view). In contrast, the religious position, as a mirror image, is precisely the expression of the annulment of denial regarding the relationship between the civil and the religious. Namely, this position embraces the civil-other towards including it, to the point of annulling its otherness, while the civil position rebuffs the religious-other to further repel its otherness. And to what side are we to attribute the present position? Does it belong particularly to the theological field in a way that does not acknowledge the autonomy of the civil, or does it dwell on the border between the two positions, since it accepts them both as being concurrently possible? It accepts both the inclusion of the civil in the religious and their independent existence, maybe because in a theoretical parallel universe, the religious may be included in the civil.

The "all". Some claim that the Israeli event in question was inspired by the global protests that originated in the Arab world and were poured into the economic and housing stress of the Israelis. But the local surplus was somewhat guised by the assumption that the protest is generated by and intended for the civil "all for all". My following questions relate to this surplus, which is characteristic of the *civil*, both as a concept as well as a social experience that bears the weight of this concept on its shoulders.

The days of the Tent Protest, with the commotion in Tel Aviv squares that reverberated throughout the entire country, were a unifying moment for all of us, as powerful as eternity itself, as if tomorrow promised to be different. Those who went out into the streets generated a storm by which they were themselves swept, a storm that in the name of housing problems, threatened to cause the collapse of the old familiar stability and recreate a new-old definition of feeling at home.

A local universal spirit borne by students and workers demanded a home, livelihood, a way out, in a self-aware confusion, made up of a double ardor – both for a physical home as well as a spiritual one, in which one feels at home.

The protest spoke of the immediate need to overturn the old social-economic order and against the domination of the neo-liberal discourse in Israel which in its imaginary past had been a socialist country (ignoring the question of which ethnic "proletarian" that country served).[13] The state – the elevated, abstract, sovereign body that draws its legitimate tangibility from the civil gaze that ratifies it – was required to serve as a home for all, both metaphorically and strictly speaking, through a new distribution of capital. Affordable housing for all, i.e., a physical home, was supposed to mark this change. To facilitate the unmediated encounter between the state and the "all", the one standing in the middle, the capitalist, was labeled the landlord, state-holder and predator. "All" was meant to include everyone, without exposing the difference, the erasure of which serves the granting of a home to each and every one.

Pointing out the "all" was meant to be the beginning of the road towards the fulfillment of the passion for a home. But pointing out the factors – namely, the state, the capitalist, and the "all" – as playing alone in the playground, in effect obstructed any real attempt to discuss the other factors on the field, i.e., both the tensions between the players themselves as well as those entangled in each one of them, notably among the "all". In this fashion, the *civil* eliminated, inter alia and perhaps especially, *the theological*, the same sphere that in effect stimulates these tensions.

From a temporal distance, the following description might seem illusionary, but to those who experienced the moment of the universal protest from within, it seemed that the current wave mixes the old cards of intra-Jewish identities, such as Mizrahi/Ashkenazi, putting together anew the field of signifiers known as *right* and *left* in anticipation to bring peace among the religious/secular and Arab/Israeli fields of identity. But the draft penetrated home, blew away its habitants confused and united under the sign "all", expecting the home-state to bestow a sense of **home** on them.

Only that as soon as the protest commenced, skeptics from both right and left began to wonder who exactly were those "all", the "we" that spoke for "all of us", protesting and sounding their voices in the name of "all".[14] Furthermore, it may be argued that it was not only the demonstration of "all" and the erasure of difference that manipulated the protest to its paralysis and self-suppression, but also that any improvement for even just a few of the all cannot be attained without exposing the secular-religious, the Jewish-Arab and the Ashkenazi-Mizrahi tensions. These tensions of identity must be acknowledged and dealt with, otherwise, they tend to obstruct the possibility to alter capitalistic priorities. The state, to which the protest was addressed, is not an anonymous face behind the curtain of citizenship but tends to understand and formulate itself under certain national-religious-identifying shades, that are usually undisguised.

If we inverse the Marxist pyramid, we could contend that the basis, the Real, is precisely the unconscious of the ideo-theo-logical that pushes the material super-structure so that the pyramid returns to its original allegedly false ideological position in space. Such formulation may provide a platform for an initial response to those supporting a certain basic position, according to which the civil-secular is a pure and neutral area, free of any religious specter, and so it is possible to instantaneously overturn the local-Zionist agenda towards its constitution as civil on a universal basis.

The new home. Yearning for a home in its natural, reassuring, pleasant sense, free of the remains of alienation, estrangement, ambivalence, and rejection, was part and parcel of the initial phantasm of the Zionist Movement, under the slogan of a return to the homeland, to the comfort of the home. This project involved de-theologization of the Jewish discourse into a national modernistic-secular and/or socialist one. The socialist (Ashkenazi) upgrade was an attempt to reclaim the pre-religious fraternity for the Jewish community, according to the phantasmatic standards of the biblical imagination.[15]

The wish was to remove the Palestinian domesticity (allegedly beyond the imaginary field, "there" in the concrete, original reality) from its Palestinian residents, to leave it Palestinian as in the imaginary Biblical times, and populate it with the Hebrew neo-Palestinian, namely, the European Jew, who bore the orientalist image of the authentic Orient. The appropriation of the Arab keffiyeh and jellabiya by the *Shomer* people [a Jewish defense organization in Palestine], for example, constituted a paradigmatic demonstration of this ideal impersonation by way of exchanging one interior for another, preserving the exterior walls and replacing the population, both in their private homes and in their homeland. The habitants were removed, and the walls were spared. Since then, the Israeli-Palestinian conflict is characterized by the preservation of the domesticity of the private home (we may recall the frequent clashes between Israel and Gaza during which Israeli missiles targeted private houses).

Back to Zionism: the passion was and still is to finally attain a stable home, not a turtle home that wanders with the Jew wherever he/she goes, but a permanent one. This yearning was provoked into action notably by the Jews entrapped in modern Europe between two impossible positions: diaspora life in the closed Ghetto (a disconnected, wandering home), or assimilation in an unwelcoming Europe - the more strongly they attempted to integrate into Christian-Western progress, the more Europe rejected them - to the culmination of the horrid, final solution. The Jew in the diaspora felt alienated and estranged from his/her own (European) home. The Unhomely (Unheimlich). The conceptual allusion brings us back to Freud's essay on *Das Unheimlich*, which was initially published in 1919, shortly after the ravages of the Great War, translated into English "The Unhomely". The essay describes the grim mental biography of the modern European man and his inability to escape the traumatic and the horrific. Freud examines a sensation that the German language well expresses, the sensation of the foreign inherent within the inti-mate itself, of chill and discomfort in the encounter with the heimlich that is at once mysterious and secret, threatening and enticing. It may be contended that in the vigorous examination of menace and alienation by the father of psycho-analysis whose Jewishness was borderline, the scientific and clinical contexts cover up first and foremost a self-perception of the wandering (European) Jew who experiences at once the comfort of the home and the anxiety of the unho-mely, the feeling of the uncanny, non-home. For Freud, this unhomely – and this is much more relevant to our investigation – expresses also the anxiety of the modern man who consciously believes in rationality and in his detachment from superstitions, but unnatural instances force him to come to terms with a spiritual and mysterious world, the theological lurking for anxiety.

The Freudian *uncanny*, the Lacanian *Real*, and the post-modern *difference* are all concepts that seek to describe our encounter with what cannot receive a stable meaning, with what is hidden in the most supposedly legible, explicit of our places – our intimate, protected home. But the unhomely is originally a psychoanalytical concept, not only philosophical, thus it is worth mentioning that for Freud, and even more so for Lacan, the is strongly connected to the castration anxiety, the experience linked to our very human deficiency, to our incapability to attain wholeness. Ultimately, our knowledge will always encoun-ter castration, the limit, the end of our world, which is also non-other than death. Even the safe havens we build for ourselves to ensure we will not get hurt or harmed, confront us at times with the horror of the unhomely, the horror of the hidden, pointing to the border and beyond it. And the most terrifying aspect of this is that what haunts us the most is not the stranger outside our home, but home itself.

In one of his lexical examples for the term *Heimlich*, Freud cites from the Bible: "He will shelter me in his pavilion on an evil day, grant me the protection of his tent, raise me high upon a rock" (*Psalms* 27: 5). The pavilion, the home, is a hiding place, a protective space, in which God houses his servant, David. But the hiding place, as such, also increases the experience of anxiety, which is central in Freud's essay. The *Unheimlich* and the *Heimlich* face each other in a mirroring game of threatening similarity, according to Freud's analysis, as follows:

> What interests us most in this long extract is to find that among its different shades of meaning the word 'heimlich' exhibits one which is identical with its opposite, 'unheimlich'. What is heimlich thus comes to be unheimlich. (Cf. the quotation from Gutzkow: 'We call it "unheimlich"; you call it "heimlich".') In general, we are reminded that the word 'heimlich' is not unambiguous, but belongs to two sets of ideas, which, without being con-tradictory, are yet very different: on the one hand it means what is familiar and agreeable, and on the other, what is concealed and kept out of sight.[1]

'Unheimlich' is customarily used, we are told, as the contrary only of the first signification of 'heimlich', and not of the second. Sanders tells us nothing concerning a possible genetic connection between these two meanings of heimlich. On the other hand, we notice that Schelling says something which throws quite a new light on the concept of the Unheimlich, for which we were certainly not prepared. According to him, everything is unheimlich that ought to have remained secret and hidden but has come to light.

[...]

Thus, heimlich is a word the meaning of which develops in the direction of ambivalence, until it finally coincides with its opposite, unheimlich. Unheimlich is in some way or other a sub-species of heimlich.[16]

Back to Zionism. Zionism wished precisely to be saved from this anxiety, to move to a non-ambivalent home, the homely home, the promised land, the normal-civil, while detaching itself from the spiritual detachment from the land, through an impossible displacement of the waiting for the Messia, through estranging estrangement, towards a physical-concrete home. Zionism sought to neutralize the land to which it aspired to return from its prior metaphysical dimension, in favor of a natural, primal, biblical, non-religious, even pre-religious, and at times Canaanite, home.

But as Gershom Scholem feared and expressed in his letter to Franz Rosenzweig from 1926, this *civil* will soon discover that the *theological*, the sanctified, refuses to be left outside and to lead a normal-civil existence:

The land is a volcano. It lodges the language. There is much talk here of many a thing that could cause our downfall. There is much talk these days particularly about the Arabs. But another danger, graver than the Arab people is threatening us, a danger forcefully brought about by the Zionist project. What will be the outcome of the Hebrew "now"? Will not the abyss of the holy language in which we have immersed our children gape its mouth?

Indeed, the people here are unaware of the ramifications of their deeds. They believe that they have transformed Hebrew into a secular language. That they have extracted from it the apocalyptic sting. But this is not so. The secularization of a language is but empty words, a figure of speech. It is not possible in effect to discharge the words that explode with significance, unless we pay the price of abandoning the language itself. Indeed, this "Wolapük", the ghostly language that we speak in the streets, represents exactly that linguistic world, void of expression, that is the only one which could perhaps be "secularized", but if we are to pass on to our children the language that was given to us, if we the middle generation revive for them the secret ancient language so that they may rediscover it – will the day not come when the religious vigor covert in it erupt against its speakers? And what character will bear the generation against which its expression will turn? For to live in this language is like living on the brink of the abyss, and most of us walk upon it blindly. Are we not facing the danger that we, or the next generation, will slide into it when we open our eyes? And there is no telling whether the sacrifice made by the few lost in that abyss will have provided an adequate cover for it. [...] Our children have no other language anymore. And the truth must be told: they, and they alone, will pay the price of the encounter that we had forced upon them without their accord, without ours. [...] The moment the power inherent in the language exposes itself, when the "spoken" - namely the content of the language - resumes a form then our people will find themselves again within a tradition in which the critical paragon is sanctification. And the people will have to choose one of the two options: either succumb or be doomed. God will not remain silent in the language in which He had been sworn thousands of times to return to our lives. The inevitable revolution of a language in which His voice is present is the one issue that is not discussed here, because the revivers of the Hebrew language did not believe in the apocalypse that their actions destined for us. If only the recklessness that has led us on this apocalyptic path will not be the ruin of us.[17]

We still speak in the same language that has not yet made up its mind whether Scholem's words to Rosenzweig were correct or not or will be so in the future; it may calm itself down or soon enough its sanctified pharynx will unleash its theological element and conquer every fraction of disbelief, whether in a good or evil spirit, through loving temptation or coercion.

If we were to exchange Scholem's metaphor of the eruption of the language from its encapsulated sanctity with the land erupting internally from an apocalyptic sanctity, underscoring his opening lines, "the land is a volcano", we might gain additional insight into the rebellion of the young generation that set camp on Rothschild Boulevard, and perceive it as the (last?) protest (or fibrillation?), whose unconscious aim was non-other than the struggle against the apocalyptic-sanctified, a struggle for social justice, for the right of "all" to have a home, for *horizontal justice*. Perhaps this was also a struggle against the apocalyptic-paranoid trend that always places the political-theological existence in the manacles of "a state of emergency".

This civil fibrillation of the young ones is at the flipside of the ominous theological. Notably, the apocalyptic threat will seize the civil when the latter exhibits tolerance toward non-Jewish-orthodox identities and minorities, which are considered by the nationalistic-theological discourse a mob on its eve of extinction. This threat was experienced by the liberal secular when God's messengers and His wrath on earth attempted to crush its symbolic home – the supreme court in Jerusalem – a few days before the great revolt (nationalist orthodox settlers from the occupied territories attacked the supreme court, which in Israel represents the establishment – the *supreme home* that protects the subject of justice - because of its alleged plotting against the settlers' houses that are driving Palestinians away from their homes).

In this respect, the civil, which aspires to normalize its "normality", is positioned nowadays in opposition to the representatives of the transcendent being and concept on earth. The subjection of those theologists to the divine transcendence and exclusiveness will impede the normal from civilizing reality; it will be dragged against its will to apocalyptic provocations against God, Jesus, or Allah (so that the vertical-divine will break free from its frustrating apathy and at long last bring the redeeming Messiah to earth).

The *Supra-homely*. The economic helplessness facing the young Israelis motivated them to protest about not being able to afford a home. To this, we might add another, interior motivation – the concrete need for a physical home with walls and rooms; a motivation that stemmed from their increasing sense of alienation. From the very start of the protest, located on Rothschild Boulevard, some identified it – rightly or wrongly so – with the stereotype of the young-secular-Tel Aviv-sushi-eating- Ashkenazi. Also, even though this sense of "all" that stirred the protest was characterized by diminishing difference and an all-civil status, their critics seemed to think that their aspirations were perfectly bourgeois[18] (the trajectory of the march of the empty baby carts, in which the author participated with his young family, ended at the central shopping mall).

Perhaps what consciously and unconsciously motivates civilians bearing this stereotypical image is the sense of affront, the loss of the sense of home, the frustration with their civil territory being menaced by the theological-sanctified-religious other, which for them signifies that Israel is no longer their home, and **in retrospect, never was.**[19] During the infinitely long weeks of the protest, we were introduced – through multiple articles in the media, especially online - to the lamentations of young people (mostly Ashkenazi, admittedly) seeking a home abroad, away from their home. The emigration of young people to Berlin was especially emphasized in these articles as if it had become a routine matter. The incinerated non-home became an alternative home.

Of the three examples cited by Freud in his article for the meaning of the word *Unheimlich*, the most central one is Schelling's, which for Freud contains the most significant components of the word: *"'Unheimlich' is the name for everything that ought to have remained ... secret and hidden but has come to light'"*;[20] does the civil repeatedly stumble upon the theological wall, the transcendent, which is perhaps a **transcendent shift to a home (world), a supra-home?**

A two-phase neologism is proposed here, a sort of hybridization of two concepts, one artificial, one natural. The first one, is Freud's invention - the *Überich* (the superego) - and the other - the *Unheimlich* - had been rooted in the German language since always and studied by Freud. In this *Supra Heimlich*, they are merged into what may be pronounced in German, *Über-Heimlich*, the stratum above the home, that which observes and controls it, thinks it, makes it what it is, strengthens and suffocates it into the most home, while infusing it with ominous anxiety.

This supra-homely collides with the civilian's normalcy in his/her non-reflexive everyday life. It is the unconscious aspect wholly conscious of the super-subject within the ideological order, the same that the state imagines itself to be. Within this dissonance, the civil subjects sense the unhomely anxiety; that the home, or about-to-become-home is shaky, mutable, uncanny, and oppressing. Their outcry is non-other than a complaint against the Other, the state, which has not been able to provide them with a clear, residue-free, secular home, does not allow its people to rest from its battles to let them have their desired peaceful atmosphere, their little Switzerland. For, the tent campers demanded nothing more than a sense of home, neither unhomely nor supra-homely, but a little peace and quiet, without an "Iron Wall" a la Jabotinsky's doctrine nor an artillery one a la Netanyahu.

Why tents? The tent expresses on the one hand fixed mobility – one that will not renounce its flexibility – and on the other, a mobile fixation: a static condition that moves from one place to another like a turtle carrying its carapace - its home – on its back. An imaginary psychologist dealing with the collective unconscious might add that this object could symbolize the very material momentariness against which the protestors protest, their inability to earn a home. But this is a symbol, a metaphor relating to the psychic aspect, not necessarily to material reality. The collective psychic has erupted against the restoration of the Jewish ancient momentariness, towards a physical home which is also a transition to a wall-like physicality, and equally a disengagement from the metaphysical home, the theological home, the one associated with the divine-vertical other which had always been an unsettling component of the Jewish collective unconscious, pushing towards an endless exile, infinite nomadism.

As **human beings**, most civilians – even when they are mindful of the other, of politics, of reflection, of their supposed internal-external-internal observance – seek not to be too divulged for themselves; they seek inner peace, are preoccupied with their own and their families' personal issues, in their homes, and do not let outsiders see the dampness of their unhomely home.[21] There are exceptions to these rules perceived by the imaginary other as existing between the beyond-human and the a-human, locked in a midpoint that is no longer an everyday human: these are the philosopher, the artist, the politician, and their likes, who are themselves locked within an intimate group, and this entire group is also tarnished by these exceptional situations so that no one remains clean.

The *familial* resents exterior interferences, seeking to remain anonymous. In a way, the screaming, whining neurotic (the protestor?) is non-other than the one whose intimate and familial have been harmed, for their home has become unhomely, *Unheimlich*, uneasy, due to an internal or mental crisis, or because an element in the family has violated the interior trust. In their essence, man and woman are motivated by the desire to conserve the interior concern, and reject the encounters with the exterior, the harassing, discomforting other, unless a crisis arises in the tranquility of the intimate; then the horizontal other – as a figure of authority or support, a prosthesis (such as the sweeping community of protestors) – is called upon to help the subject realize his/her ambition. There is a danger that this other, which is in effect the phantasmatic of the *theological* (as other towards being absolute and vertical), will subjugate the ego (because the other tends to slide towards this subjugating situation, this interpellation of what is already- always a subject towards being a subject; Lacan attempted to free the other from this fixation and thereby the analyst from identifying with it).

Moreover, the protest merged the intimate need for a home and the demand for social justice, the bourgeois longing for a home, for a non-dialectic privacy, for the individualism of the specific home with the demand for affordable housing for all; in the background, the civil discourse was but the one summoning the struggle for the personal while positioning it under the general, abstract concept of the subject.

These civilians, each one in her/his own way, came together via the field of the other, which is but a compound of the *all*, as a dimension of generalized transcendence and one seeking to be civil and neutralized from the impact of the divine other of absolute justice. Notwithstanding, there were a few infiltrators from the rightwing and the orthodoxy who joined in, but their influence was marginal and included some slogans for achieving justice "according to the prophets' tradition". In contrast, the protestors' attitude towards the religious discourse was blatantly reduced to arguments referring to the orthodoxy's exploitation of the state treasury, arguments which may be perceived as neo-anti-Semitic, regardless of whether they are true or false. This current discussion of critical theology seeks to crack both facets and confront them with the real of their other.

Critical Theology? When such an Israeli attempt rises to claim a home but also to regain the *sense of home*, we have to wonder about the position of the *civil* vis-à-vis the *theological*, which has also become nationalist (and therefore perceives the state as uniquely its own and others as visitors, at best). Is a civil revolution that will totally dismiss the theological aspect of our lives possible, considering that we are ostensibly atheists?

Perhaps there is another way. Is critical theology at all possible? An unlikely, utopian possibility perhaps, for we are aware that not much sustains this naïve belief about the possibility to change the discourse of the theological as such, when it presents itself as rigid, guarded, and impermeable. The same goes for the likelihood to change the civil discourse which is also becoming more and more rigid within its own limited vicinity.

This could be however a novel (a-)theology that is not vociferous towards its protected sanctity but fragmented and pulverized. Does the situation allow for critical work that would take away from the Jewish theology its self-confidence, its sense of home, introducing unfamiliarity into it, reconstituting it, while reconstituting the theological-national-mythical field, in order to extricate from it a deeper, truer dimension which in its beginning was but civil pre-political – a phantasmatic beginning but nonetheless a living concrete one? In question is the very human horizon expressed in the primal biblical ethos, in the elegy of the destruction of God's Temple, analogous to the loss of the private home and of the civil sense of home in Canaan long ago.[22]

People in the Israeli political center-left understand in their heart of hearts that the moment to exhaust their ideas about changing the civil-economic sta-tus-quo, as well as resolving the Israeli-Palestinian conflict, is drawing close. Despite the persistence of the obsessive attempts to dismantle power relations, and the belief in creative solutions for one-state for all its citizens, in which friends and foes would live together, in which the tensions and the differences will be obliterated, all of these are perceived as utopian means and ends that bear no relationship whatsoever to the political reality.

There exists both an intended and unintended opacity (not necessarily blindness) regarding the roots of these conflicts and the feasibility for a redeem-ing shift, for the problem is not solely political. These conflicts, *at least* as far as the situation in Israel is concerned, are rooted in the mythical-theological field. Hence, a shift will materialize only in the same super-narrative. Not in its regularization, annulment, or modulation into a "healthier" plane, but through animating its sometimes-liberating potential. We have neglected the ancient mythos whose center is an ethos of subjugation to the transcendent dimension and succumbed to the elements that provoke the various conflicts in ways that do not advance them towards an ethical solution. Now is the time to choose a different path. The solution lies in the reconstitution of the entire mythic con-figuration by finding a new key that will alter the entire field of signification (according to Lacan's concept of *quilting point* [*point de capiton*], found between the field of meaningless-empty-field of signifiers-utterances and the field of meaning/signified, a shift of which may produce a whole new existential mean-ing to the patient/subject's discourse). Namely, if the arena is ethnic-national-ist-aggressive, we may bring in universal, liberating principles, but back them up with a new key that will alter the entire field of identifications, by reconsti-tuting it; a key that will entice the theological to generate its own interior change, from within itself, paving its way to the civil.

Notes

1 [Jacque Lacan during the debate hosted by the French Society of Philosophy on the 22nd on February, 1969, with M. Foucault, M. de Gandillac, L. Goldman, J. d'Ormesson, J. Ullmo, and J. Wahl. In the English translation of Foucault's lecture, the above passage has been omitted. I therefore translated it from the original French: Michel Foucault, *Qu'est-ce qu'un auteur* (Bulletin de la Société française de philosophie, 63 anné, no 3, juillet-septembre 1969), pp. 73-104. Translator's note. All the translator's notes will appear in square parantheses].

2 [The protest was instigated by the rise of the cost of the cottage cheese, an Israeli symbol. Therefore, it received the name "The Cottage Protest". The author here plays with the Hebrew expression "Crème children", - children of wealthy families - and terms them "Cottage cheese children"].

3 Max Weber, *The Protestant Ethic and the Spirit of Capitalism*, transl. Talcott Parsons (Los Angeles: Roxbury Publishing Company, 1998).

4 To paraphrase Walter Benjamin's thought on the mystical element of the law, and Jacques Derrida's response to his discussion. See Walter Benjamin, "Critique of Violence", in Benjamin, *Selected Writings Vol. 1 1913-1926*, ed. M. Bullock and M. Jennings (Cambridge, MA: Harvard University Press, 1996), 236-252; Jacques Derrida, "Force of the Law: The Mystical Foundation of Authority", in *Deconstruction and the Possibility of Justice*, ed. D. Cornell, M. Rosenfeld, D. Gray Carlson (New York and London: Routledge, 1992), 3-67.

5 To some extent, Durkheim's thesis concurs with thinking about the social via Freud's working through in *Totem and Taboo*, i.e. working through the fatherly vertex of the social-religious, the singular figure to which the social-religious experience is channeled. See, Émile Durkheim, *The Elementary Force of the Religious Life*, transl. Joseph Ward Swain (Mineola, NY: Dover Publications, 2008). Durkheim's text was one of the cornerstones in Freud's theory in *Totem and Taboo*.

6 Étienne Balibar, *Citizen Subject: Foundations for Philosophical Anthropology*, transl. Steven Miller (New York: Fordham University Press, 2016).

7 Jean-Jacques Rousseau, *On The Social Contract*, ed. Roger D. Masters, transl. Judith R. Masters (New York: St. Martin's: 1978).

8 See for example the discussions on the relationship between the symbolic order and the subject, in Jacques Lacan, *The Seminar of Jacques Lacan, Book II: The Ego in Freud's Theory and in the Technique of Psychoanalysis*, transl. Sylvana Tomaselli (New York: W.W. Norton, 1991).

9 See Lacan's discussion in lessons 6-9, Book XI of his Seminar on the gaze (*regard*), as opposed to seeing (*voir*), which characterizes the presence of the ominous Other vis-a-vis the subject. In this sense, the subject is always the object of the object/ other. See, Jacques Lacan, *The Seminar of Jacques Lacan, Book XI: The Four Fundamental Concepts of Psychoanalysis*, transl. Alan Sheridan (New York: W.W. Norton, 1998). See also Freud's description of the shadow that falls upon the self in the case of melancholia: Sigmund Freud, *Mourning and Melancholy*, SE, transl. James Strachey (London: Hogarth Press).

10 Compare with Freud's conception of denial and repression. In most of his writings, Freud underscores the effective mechanism of repression as constructing the logic of the unconscious and is contained in it. Denial is described in Freud's essay "Fetishism". Freud differentiates between the repression that occurs in the affective domain and the consciousness' non-recognition of something the eye captured, such as in the case of the child that denies his mother's castration, albeit seeing her genitals. Lacan viewed repression as the central mechanism of the neurotic and denial as the central mechanism of negation in perversions.

11 Jacques Lacan, *Ecrits*, transl. Bruce Fink (NY and London: W.W Norton, 2006) (2002), 364.

12 Ariel Hendel et al, eds., *Kriat Hameha'a: Lexicon Politi* [*The voice of Protest: A Political Lexicon*] (Tel Aviv: Hakibbutz Hameuhad, 2011), 139.

13 Regarding the fight of the middle class in the neoliberal discourse as part of the protest, see Uri Ram and Dani Filc: "The 14th of July of Dafni Leef: The Rise and Fall of the Social Protest" in *Forum: The Social Protest*, ed. by Uri Ram and Dani Filc, *Theory and Criticism 41*, 2013: 17-44 [in Hebrew].

14 See for example Boaz Piler's article on Ynet: "The Protestors of Rothschild are Rejoicing: All of Israel Together" https://www.ynet.co.il/articles/0,7340,L-4108298, 00.html [in Hebrew].

15 Regarding the Zionist political theology, see for example the sharp presentation of Hannan Hever "Introductory Notes" in his book, *With the power of God: Theology and Politics in Modern Hebrew Literature* (Bnei Brak: Hakibutz Hameuhad, 2013 [in Hebrew]).

16 Sigmund Freud. The Uncanny (1919), SE 17, pp. 223-225.

17 Gershom Scholem, "Hatzharat Emunim Lasafa Shelanu" ("Declaration of Faith to our Language"), *Od Davar* (Tel Aviv: Am Oved, 1989 [in Hebrew]). The letter was written in Jerusalem in January 1926.

18 One protestor from Tel Aviv wrote: "I have a good job, a sound salary. I am a typical Tel Avivian, in the middle, from the middle class, but I deserve more. I'm not asking for anything for free, and I wish for my parents to age with dignity"; the organizer of the wagons protest wrote: "We all need a home, we all need education, we need to know that raising children in this country is not a second mortgage. We are sick and tired of the disproportion between our incomes and the cost of living". See Roi Mendel and Roi Kaise "Thousands are Protesting in the Baby Carts Protest: Bibi Go Home." Published on Ynet, 28.7.2011. DOI: https://www.ynet.co. il/articles/0,7340,L-4101470,00.html.

19 See Yotam Hotem, "Judocrathy", in HaEmory Blog. https://haemori.wordpress. com/2011/08/30/judocrac/.

20 Sigmund Freud. The Uncanny (1919), SE 17: 225.

21 See Eric Santner's commentary on Franz Rosenzweig's position towards the inability of the dyad to open up to a triad and its pertinence to the relations between the Jewish people and its God and the inability to express it in the "mitzvah". Santner associates this position with Lacan's *Real* and *Traumatic*. Eric L. Santner, *On the Psychotheology of Everyday Life: Reflections on Freud and Rosenzweig* (Chicago: Chicago University Press, 2001).

22 The Bible Studies scholar, Edward Greenstein, singles out the trauma of the Babylon Exile as a source of understanding the whole Biblical corpus, at least as far as the unique position of the editor/s of the Cannon goes, during the period of the Second Temple. See, Edward L. Greenstein, "The Torah as She is Read", *Response* 47 (Winter 1985): 17-40.

Chapter 4

The Israeli Anxiety
With Freud, Heidegger, Lacan, and Netanyahu[1]

We deliver the words that have been dormant amidst us thus far, existing for themselves alone, enveloped in an elevated abstract philosophical language, lazy, fearing a possible encounter with the *Id*, what Freud called in Yiddish, *dreck*. They are going out into the world, not entirely confident of their coherence, even forfeiting such coherence that might lead to failure, so we may feel this infinitely intricate "thing" accumulated in a single word, "Israel."

We aim to point a hermeneutical finger at the thingness of this thing in the Heideggerian sense of the term: "*[...] das Dingsein (die Dingheit), des Dinges*,"[2] namely, to encounter the thingness of the word "Israel" itself (and Israel-as-a-word), as a thing, as being, and not just as a concept, namely, not as the idea of the significance of the word, or its content for us, or the public discourse but as an object-in-itself and not necessarily one subjected to our own gaze or to our object of subjectivity. Instead, *we* are its object, Israel's objects, in the most tangible sense.

We aim to attain the thing-concept, which produces anxiety in the subject, that thing that belongs to it in the most intimate manner, as part of the subject's experience – particularly in the subject's bodily extension – of confronting the unbearable non-definition between the pure concept and the pure thing. Moreover, we shall lead the Heideggerian thought of the concept to the doorway of Freud's psychoanalytical configuration of the thing in the *Project for a Scientific Psychology*,[3] as well as to Lacan's Seminar *VII: Ethics of Psychoanalysis*[4] (who, contrary to the current neurological tendency to explain anxiety as a neuronic failure which can be medicated, explores the most neglected thing textually and transforms it into the fulcrum of his and Freud's doctrine). Then, the thing receives the angle of anxiety.

Since our hermeneutical deliberation refers to the thing and the encounter between the thing and the subject, the modern traditional western hermeneutics underlying the rupture in the current discussion is worth mentioning.

DOI: 10.4324/9781003667339-4

This tradition originated among the German-Christian Romantics, from Schleiermacher to Heideggerian Gadamer,[5] focusing on the circularity of the subject vis-à-vis the text (our mention of them being Christians is not superfluous, for what is the New Testament if not the testament of circularity and closure in its attempt to follow the insolubility of the impossible, Old Testament?). In this circularity, the subject subjects the object-word to himself, namely, making it a subject. Moreover, it seems that in his later works on hermeneutics, Heidegger seeks to go beyond and achieve the presence of the one being present through language.[6] This presence is no other than the presence of horror and danger, which expresses a knowledge that exceeds the perception of the hermeneutical circle: according to this perception, it is precisely the object that objectifies the subject, making it his own under the hold of anxiety, as conceived by Lacan.[7]

In our case, it is the words-things "Israel" and "Israeliness" that constitute the object of the Real that burdens the subject with anxiety; our expression, "the Israeli anxiety," will not only speak of the tension inherent in the Israeli experience but also, through a terrible loop, of the Israeliness as an object of anxiety.

The expression "the Israeli anxiety" reflects, in fact, two possible hierarchical modes of comprehension. As such, we have a common constitution of our understanding of the thing-like concept as a conceptual element that affects the body materially with anxiety. This is the horrifying knowledge that stresses the body-soul. This expression may be construed linguistically as a juxtaposition:

The Israeli anxiety, in the sense of the anxiety **pertaining** to being Israeli, as a thing characterizing Israeliness.

And less in the sense of

Anxiety from the Israeliness, albeit this inferior element in the semantic hierarchy, may perhaps express a more profound and unexpected truth regarding the sense of horror concerning Israeliness itself. These two significations may merge and instruct us on the thingness of the Israeliness, whether the horror is related to it or exists within it.

Concerning the thing-like concept, it is worth noting that the Hebrew "Davar" (thing), as Ding, also signifies "Dibur" (speech), or object, meaning the logos at our fingertips. We are faced with a thing containing a certain thingness in its most concrete sense. This is not merely a conceptual essence wandering within the symbolic order of communication, thought, or literature, but rather a living reality that bears an affective dynamic in the Freudian sense.

This reality of our current moment constantly shapes the primary concept delivered by the word, as the phenomenon inscribed under this particular word, "Israel." As a mother word, endowed with adjectival ramifications, it produces identities such as "Israeli," "Israeliness," and so forth. This principal word also signifies multiple, annexed identities, which it either produces or accepts their requests to exist under its inscription: Mizrahi, Ashkenazi, Arab Israeli, Palestinian Israeli, Jewish Israeli, and so forth. Moreover, the identities constituted or signified by this word bear a real vitality that goes beyond imagination. They embody active living beings.

This vitality pushes off the assumption of the virtuality of the thing and of it being a product of mere ideological and conceptual inventions. We are left with a thing in the most object-like sense. And there is something of the real and the concrete in these identity-beings.

This is particularly demonstrated at the psycho-physical level when we address the reality of the anxiety that shapes "Israel" and its offspring as thing-like-word/s. The word "Israel" carries on its back today many of the characteristics of the thing "Israel" – be they cultural, religious, political, social, historical, or metaphysical – as a current being. We would like to get reacquainted, through new words, with the everyday living essence of "Israel," or other daughter-words, such as "Israeliness," "Israeli," and so forth, deriving from the mother-word "Israel."

The attempt to understand the complexity of the thing "Israel" compels us to restore the bustling complexity of the thingness of the word "Israel" to its current meanings, at least in the Israeli scene itself. We are faced with the hustle and bustle of Israeliness, circularly experiencing itself through its interlocutors, they alone comprehending the depth of its experience. These significations bear a particular understanding of Israeliness, while this word does not profess more than to describe some inherent essence related to Israel: that there is something of an Israeli experience, there is Israeli vitality, there is an Israeliness inherent in the Israeli.

But we are also faced with the challenge to confront this realization with the psycho-physical anxiety that is at the base of its thing-like concreteness, notwithstanding all cultural, political, and religious maneuvers and attempts to achieve an embellishing and ideal deviation from this materiality.

In this sense, it is worth pointing out that in the present text, we are submerged in hermeneutical autism assembled in its entirety around the central expression suggested here in the thingness of our thing, "the Israeli anxiety," which we attempt to fathom as if it were the only expression on earth.

Therefore, we intentionally ignore questions relating to Judaism, Jews, and affective and identifying dynamics, for they have lost their autonomy long ago. From the moment they embarked on the illegal immigration ships (in Hebrew called "Ha'Maapilim"), they sank into the deep waters with their old anguishes and were reborn into a different kind of anxious thingness driven by the materiality of the letters comprising the word "Israeliness."

Moreover, the signifier in this respect is not the original significance, or in our case, the Jewish one waiting there, but the independent sonic materiality in its material thingness, as Lacan formulates it when discussing the Instance of the Letter in his 1957 article published in the *Ecrits*:

> By "letter," I designate the material medium [support] that concrete discourse borrows from language. This simple definition assumes that language is not to be confused with the various psychical and somatic functions that serve it in the speaking subject. The primary reason for this is that language, with its structure, exists prior to each subject's entry into it at a certain moment in his mental development.
>
> [...]
>
> And the subject, while he may appear to be the slave of language, is still more the slave of a discourse in the universal movement of which his place is already inscribed at his birth, if only in the form of his proper name.[8]

In our context, the proper name is "Israel," in its most thing-like sense and in the sense that effaces its neighboring signifiers, such as "Jewish," the most. From this aspect, "Jewish" is already always in the shadow of the signifier "Israeli," which also applies to Jews or Jewish entities who do not necessarily live in the Middle East.

From this perspective, reflecting upon the ancient signification of the signifier "Israel" is not relevant here either, even though such a discussion might have poetic appeal. We remain with the materiality of the letter at its real, recalcitrant, rigid level, which will not bend to moderation, cultural constructions, or relativism. And this *Real* is the one side of the Möbius strip that has on its other side *the Symbolic* and *the Imaginary* (on this surface, the language, the side, is folded in an unusual way so that it comprises a singular circular trajectory, and when walked upon, it feels like we are moving along both its sides as it were, even though we kept walking on the same side of language).

Envisaging our trans-final thought of the thing in the era of Foucault and Deleuze, when everything is understood as fluid, relative, transgendered, trans-cybernetic, and trans-ethnic, does not seem to be a simple task. But the *Trump* thing (in American English, free of the German-Bavarian origin of Donald Trump's grandfather: hooligan, cool) is proof of the current stubborn resistance to this fluidity, in the same manner that for Lacan, the material letter is an instance – in the sense of both persistence as well as law.[9]

In addition, and without contradicting the abovesaid, this fluidity is **equally real** and dreadful, for it is positioned vis-à-vis a rigid materiality, which is not open to any dialectical or rhizomatic negotiation. Thus, it is only fitting that we also perceive the Israeliness as a wholly new and material letter, apart from its dialectical tension concerning Judaism, as complex or as impossible as this may be. The letter that kills, in the Paulinian sense.

There is that which refuses to exist as part of a metaphysical system. Hence, it is not subject to deconstruction in the Derridean sense. It is what Derrida himself maintains in *The Gift of Death*[10] regarding the intrinsic tension in monotheism and the anxiety of the sacrifice. But we speak of a real that differs from the Jewish anxiety supposed by the Jewish philosopher.

Moreover, this is not to say that there is a thingness of the nothing, lying independently behind the symbolic-structural or *the Imaginary* pertaining to the most incongruent of significations. Nor that behind the Israeli anxiety lies the nothing, that the nothing is there as a *Ding-an-sich*; but that the nothing, or the being of the nothing as thing, acts as thingness pertaining to the thing of the self for and in itself, a very personal real, indeed intimate. Such is also in relation to the thingness-of-nothing "behind" the concept "Israeli," for it does not escape its self-constitution as such, insofar as it is serious in its symbolic layer and imbecilic from a Lacanian point of view in simulating the significances of that nothing.

This conceptual work, which we have chosen to define as trans-sophy of the thing and thingness, is equally valid concerning the concepts of various thinkers as there is not necessarily a meaning given to us to assemble but rather one that is being inscribed into our discourse, and into the Israeli situation, which emanates from the status of the writer as an Israeli – an anxious-Israeli – and the status of the written as inscribing the universe as Israeli anxiety.

As we shall attempt to show, the anxiety in question is the one termed by Freud as *Realangst*: the anxiety of the real regarding the fear and helplessness against an impending threat from the exterior world.[11]

But this formulation is insufficient, for it concerns the fear of *the Real*, the thingness of the reality, the real that is present but is not easy to discern. In this respect, Israeliness recognizes the threats that always haunt its existence. Still, the anxiety referred to herein relates to a real far more menacing than the military, security-linked threats and those associated with the ongoing conflict with the Palestinian neighbors or what is perceived as an ever-increasing internal enemy. It is the real, which is the other side of the Israeli Möbius strip, the other side of the joyful pleasure.

We might add that the Real also impinges upon the enemy's expansion and not on its actual existence. The wars with the enemy camouflage a much greater horror. Hence, the constant need to always maintain a conflict on the back burner, sufficiently contained so that the aspect of camouflaging will be preserved, for the camouflage must primarily disguise the very fact of its being a camouflage. It masks itself and only then its object. Namely, the war camouflages itself as a means of camouflage and therefore must not exaggerate in this dimension; only later does it camouflage the terrifying nothing, which causes anxiety.

Perhaps we must also bear in mind that these vortexes of anxiety are also comic to a large extent, from the intra-Israeli perspective. The director of the screwball Israeli comedy *Halfon Hill Doesn't Answer* (1976), Assi Dayan, the oedipal son of General Moshe Dayan, had one of the film characters mouthing: "On the map we see Egypt, and there's Israel... the **so-called** state."

It means that the reserve duty soldier serving the Israeli army during a military clash in the Sinai desert between Israel and Egypt perceives Israel as a pseudo-state with a pseudo-border. This entire pseudo-existence oscillates between the anxiety from the war and the comic situation, in which only the Mizrahi soldiers are capable of discarding the Ashkenazi terror and melancholy. We will return to the Mizrahim later on.

In any event, it is not the anxiety vis-à-vis the object that is in question but the anxiety facing the movement of the object. Anxiety, as explained by Freud in his article "Inhibition, Symptom and Anxiety" (1926), is not related to the biological tensions of the subject but the dread associated with the disappearance of the object.[12]

However, as Lacan underscores, it is not a symbolic object but a real one, the anxiety being the collision of the objectality of the object of *the Real* with its thingness, which is the living force of the object thing, the living force of the nothing whose energy is too existent.[13] In his discussion of *Angst*, Lacan follows Heidegger:

> Anxiety is indeed anxiety in the face of... but not in the face of this or that thing. Anxiety in the face of... is always anxiety concerning... but not concerning this or that. The indeterminateness of that in the face of which and concerning which we become anxious is no mere lack of determination but rather the essential impossibility of determining it. In the following familiar phrase this indeterminateness comes to the fore. [...] Anxiety makes manifest the thing[14]

However, the nothing in hand is not an abstract nothing but a concrete nothing pertaining to an individual subject or subjectivity. It is not some generic *Dasein* of some generic *Sein*, but one that is submerged in a very particular thingness (is there anything more universal-generic, rather than particular, than existential philosophy in its diverse forms?). This thing-like particularity is the home of its nothing. In our case, this thing-like particularity is the essence of Israeliness, which is concurrently the being and the nothing, in a tension that constructs the *Unheimlich*, as embodied in Freud's and Heidegger's texts.

Furthermore, Israel's material complexity originates primarily in its dominant component, which is a political one. But this concept, in its most fundamental sense, is the existence of a state bearing the name the State of Israel. The moment of the establishment of the State of Israel is the moment of establishing the Israeli being, the concept word crystallizing to a single experience that which was initially constructed from the Jewish experience that began to settle in Palestine.

This word transformed a particular coming-into-being, which originated in the persecution and anxiety of the Jews in the hostile diaspora, into a supposedly extra-anxiety being and not supposedly into a counter-anxiety entity. Hence, the word "Israel" figures as a state, a word that underwent a rebirth, effacing the old traumatic significances it had borne from the ancient biblical world. This word has been the true basis of the "etymology" of the Israeli experience from that moment onward. This concrete etymology may also instruct us on what has ensued, the various reincarnations of anxiety and extra-anxiety, insofar as it is not less real nor less affective (and even more) than anxiety in its psycho-physical corporeality.

And suppose we ponder for a moment upon the etymology of the word etymology. In that case, we may demonstrate how extricating the veritable origin of the very procedure of the word etymology may liberate it from its idealistic comprehension and lead it to its material comprehension, untangling it from the hermeneutical circularity, in which the idealistic awareness takes us back to a supposed original meaning that only reinforces the present one. And here, we refer to the Greek sense of the word, ἐτυμολογία (etumología), namely the study of the real (as opposed to truth, the study of the real beyond its ideal truth), in the sense of the essentiality of the ancient primal layer of the word, not just as a spiritual creature but also as an entirely thing-like one.

For us, the political etymology of "Israel" is not the study of a linguistic origin of the truth but an origin as an affective truth of the word, a source that is linked to the re-foundation of the word Israel as "State," a foundation that assumes the anxiety of subjectivity of the Jew defending himself in his progression toward a whole new dimension. This is not a translation but a displacement estranging from the origin, lacking any real repression. We are not facing repression of the origin but rather its evident cancellation.

Such a comprehension of foundationalism will remove us from the circularity of Israel–Israeliness as a cultural being without any disturbing effect, advanced by numbing political and capitalistic forces, which continually attempts to be found while eliminating or at least reducing the historical discontent.

From this aspect, we have to ponder on the essence of the materiality of anxiety mainly through its incarnation on the deep cultural level, even though the cultural order is seeking to present itself as extra-anxiety and pleasurable, namely as an "Israeli" who is mainly understood as liberated, light-hearted, not anxious, fun, and unrestrained. This is linked to the circular hermeneutical game in which Israel=Israeli=Israeliness, by which each individual defines his/her Other conceptually free of any threatening exterior from the linguistic, historical, and psychological points of view. This circularity is what annihilates the discontent and the tangibility of anxiety inherent in the nucleus of the Israeli.

Take a seat in chef Eyal Shani's "Miznon" (literally "Buffet") and help yourselves to authentic Israeli street food, a simulacrum of Mizrahi and Ashkenazi food integrated into a puzzle of noisy authenticity and apparent uncontrollable chaos, and you will experience circular fun: Israeliness.

We imagine an Israeli psyche being embodied in the same Israeli culture. A psyche, both in the sense of the sum of the individual psyches and the general psyche constituting the Israeliness. We believe that this same culture is ingrained in an anxious psyche but constructed in the complete Freudian sense by both camouflaged and embodied anxiety.

Of course, the state of this psyche is linked to the history of that essence. However, it is not the history of past events but one that the present constructs as a cultivated past that returns to shape the present.[15] As Lacan presumed, this is precisely why it is difficult to break free from this loop. This tension does not stem simply from repressing a past truth. We do not adhere to the simplistic notion of exposing the truth of the past. There is no past but only the present puddle and its fancies regarding its history and its future (we propose the puddle metaphor so that we may discuss the existence of the monadic subject as a closed consciousness in which the supposedly external objects are also submerged with internal tensions. There is no real exteriority but just simulations of exteriority and simulations of interiority within this puddle of subjectivity. The thought of the pool and its internal tensions may coexist with the Kleinian theory).

But before we move on to the nucleus of anxiety, we better address the identity structure of the Israeli scene, as this structure exposes even further the affective dynamics of the Israeli subject and her/his Israeliness.

This scene comprises numerous components that together constitute the mother concept of Israeliness. But these many components within the structure are actually preserving it precisely from within their continuous battles against each other. So far, the structure is stable and does not overflow its borders, nor does it annul the very definition of Israeliness, even though various axes in this tension are in constant dispute not only regarding the same pertinence and definition of the essence of Israeliness but also regarding the legitimacy of the universal Israeliness (vis-à-vis its minorities).

In light of the events that have transpired in the last decades, which include a debate regarding the definition of the essence of Israeliness, we could suggest that the question of the definition is pertinent to our discussion, for it is contiguous with another question related to the anxious subject. Who is anxious? When we say that Israelis suffer from anxiety, do we mean all Israelis, including the Palestinian Israelis? The Mizrahi ones?

So here we reverse the terms of the formula:

We are not moving from the question of the definition to the question of anxiety,

but perhaps to:

The question of anxiety precedes the question of definition.

Perhaps the question of who is the one who is anxious shapes the question of who the Israeli is. Hence, it also shapes that thing-like structure whose thing-like glue seems to be that same anxiety. This glue is made of all the tangible components of *the trauma*: the constant security threat, and mainly, the catastrophic nothing well-hidden behind the discussions and actions related to warfare. Even the arguments about Iran and all sorts of nuclear bombs will not succeed in camouflaging the camouflage behind such trivial nothing.

We do not have a home.
We do not have a home, nor shall we ever have one. This is the fundamental component of the Freudian *unheimlich* (uncanny), the tension between "un" and "heimlich" [homely and un-homely] when the inner home itself is foreign: thus, heimlich is a word, the meaning of which develops in the direction of ambivalence until it finally coincides with its opposite, unheimlich. Unheimlich is in some way or other a subspecies of heimlich.[16]

Does this mean that the "un" is the home and the nothing is the thingness of the thing Israeliness? In effect, this is a tricky question, for it supposes an **answer** where there is none. The answer to the question is the **question** itself. This question, and the impossibility of defining it, is precisely the **thingness** of the thing that engages our mind so earnestly.

This real logic is demonstrated in the first chapter of the second season of the Israeli television series *Zaguri Empire* (2015). The creator of the series, Maor Zaguri, identifies himself and is recognized by others as Mizrahi and Moroccan. He writes provocative lines for the character of the Mizrahi Moroccan father who refuses to stand at the siren commemorating the Holocaust victims, refusing to take part in the collective act of anxiety that establishes the circularity of an anxious community. For the suffering father, the questions of definition and identity and of who and what is the Israeli are closely linked to the question of what anxiety is and who is anxious as it has to do with them and not me, the Mizrahi, not to my personal trauma as an illegal immigrant sailing in the Egoz ship, suffering from the treatment of the young Ashkenazi state toward me. The question is: do I collaborate with the victimized "Ashkenazi" Holocaust anxiety or do I adopt my own victimized status, constructing my Israeliness henceforth not around their victimization but mine, around **my own nothing**.

This proves how much nothing is present and how much it exists.

But this issue goes deeper than the mere appropriation of victimization or the Holocaust. It refers to the appropriation of **what is impossible to appropriate**:

The Real

The unattainable and the inconceivable that really define Israeliness
    And if there is an imaginary schema, then it will be

real **nothing** > anxiety > identity > Israeliness

So here, to achieve the state of being Israeli, one must act in order to acquire the original

nothing

And again, this **nothing** does not really exist by itself, but it is a

nothing that exists **in itself-for** the subject

The **existing-nothing** of the Israeli being is the Holocaust. It is the most solid existence. And most of the identities and sub-identities are organized around it as a form of terrifying *Das Ding*. Even the most radical and the most anti-Zionist of Palestinians are entangled in this self-definition vis-à-vis the thingness of the Holocaust. Not really the thing, but its thingness, its extracted fluid that loiters around all. Thus, for example, the Palestinians are trading their nothing for the nothing of the Holocaust based on the following equivalents:

Nakba = Shoah >>>> our Shoah **instead** of your Shoah + our Shoah **instead** of the Nakba

The "instead" is the kernel of the Palestinian subjectivity, more so even than the Nakba itself, which can only express itself as

the thing in itself for the subject

Understandably, this is also manifested in young Israelis for whom Auschwitz is the kernel of Israeliness, not Judaism.

But Auschwitz conceals something else.

Not the nothing but mainly the fact that **it is concealing**

For the subject, this is the most unbearable, most aporetic real,

Is this repression? Perverse denial? Psychotic foreclosure? For Lacan, repression is a neurotic act vis-à-vis signifiers, and anxiety exists vis-à-vis something that goes beyond repression, something that has no signifier but whose territory is the thing and thingness.

In our case, we argue that the Israeli thing is the real thing of the Israeli anxiety, the subject and object of the same question, the anxious and anxiety and the anxiety and the object of anxiety. For what reason? Because the formation of the subject in his/her Israeli existence begets him/her, his/her impossible terms of possibility, and his/her finiteness, more remarkably than in other analogous situations in any other national or conceptual system, be it American, European, or Palestinian.

Moreover, and perhaps in contrast with the above contention, our attempts to touch upon the essence of this real will encounter what seems as repression of elements, such as holocaust-nothing-home. There seems to be something more problematic linked to the Möbius strip's problematic structure: the most horrific real is the real that is bare, in the sense of the thingness of the thing mentioned above, thus infiltrating *the Symbolic* and/or *the Imaginary*.[17] As far as we are concerned, it is the very non-anxious state of Israeliness that is, in fact, *the Real*. Wait. In effect, this is really not the *Real* either, but the real is the actual Möbian act of **multiplication**. Or is it?

To touch upon these disconcerting questions, not necessarily with the aim of understanding them or answering them in an erudite manner, we must again touch upon how the various conflicted identities compete against each other for belonging to, animosity towards, appropriation of, or inclusion in the Israeliness. For, as far as the question of anxiety is concerned, we must consider that there exists a sort of **overdetermination** – in the Freudian, and to a certain extent in the Althusserian, sense of the term *Uberdeterminierung* – of Israeli identities that perceive themselves as superior vis-à-vis other Israeli identities (the superiority and inferiority being a matter of self-perception and not of historical truth, for the nationalistic right in Israel has been in power for quite a few decades, but surprisingly enough perceives itself as being oppressed by the Ashkenazi, secular, and quite imaginary elite).

In the practice of overdetermination, there are two fields, each one of them comprising innumerable factors, so that in each area, each element entertains relations with a certain number of elements of the other field. In effect, the dream created under this over-causality principle envelops a real in a complicated, obscured manner. Much like the dream of the burning child, which hides something more real, more disturbing than the dream itself, but at the same time protects from it.[18]

We may also envisage this dreaminess through the term "**fractal**": sub-categories such as Arab, Mizrahi, and Jewish are constructed along with the relations of over-causality with those under them in the hierarchy of identity, in the very same manner in which they interact hierarchically with those above them under the logic of over-causality. Hence, in the dreamy situation of Israeliness, we receive each of the categories within a network of overdetermination. There is a tangled network of relationships between various identity groups, such as Western identities versus Oriental ones. But, as mentioned above, structurally, each group comprises in a fractal mode structurally inferior relations with those who have the same tensions pertaining to the logic of over-causality. Such a labyrinth is inescapable; thus, our only choice is to experience the permanent state of the Israeli anxiety within it. Indeed, in the network constituted by the overdetermination of various types of anxiety and their extensions, between the anxieties and the multiple identities, in this entire network of disorder, there is the master-signifier, the Name-of-the-Father of Israeliness that is holding the whole network together, but only through the tension of the anxiety that knows no self-exhaustion.

So far, we have been describing various identity traits that compete against each other within the space of Israeliness, mainly for the treasures of pain and oppression:

- Ashkenazi and Mizrahi on **the Holocaust, immigration and oppression, and cultural competition**
- Arab and Jews on **the Nakba and the Holocaust and issues of disparity**
- Leftists and rightists on **the Occupation**
- Moroccans versus all other Mizrahi Jews on **who has been more oppressed by the establishment**
- The Druze versus all other Israelis on the **death of Druze soldiers in action as justifying the granting of rights**
- Foreign workers versus the government on **how much they have really suffered in their African countries of origin, and to what extent are they worthy of being defined as refugees and not merely foreign workers.**

The trauma and nullification are generated within a continuous attempt to appropriate the annulment and empower through the protrusion of the nullifying trauma that becomes an asset and a source of reinforcement.

The trauma is nullifying indeed and in a real manner, for the subject complaining of his/her suffering may be oblivious to the fact that the very oppression itself is what had constituted his/her subjectivity. As if the slightest offense toward this vulnerability incorporates a danger of nullifying the subject (this may infer that the traumatic nothing is preferable to any violation of the traumatic-victim status and the very traumatic experience threatening nullification). This is the threat of *the Real*. Not a physical threat, but a threat in the most Lacanian sense of the term, for the subject cannot contain it and will therefore continue to circle the **circles of complaint** against the oppressive *Other* (who, in effect, is also responsible for his/her creation as such!).

Therefore, we are facing once again the Israeli thing, which is itself *the Real*, so that the Israeli thing is both *the Symbolic* and *the Real* concurrently. It seems that the Spinozian metaphor regarding God and Nature may apply here as an allegory: God is *the Symbolic*, while Nature is *the Real*.

Moreover, the realness of the real thing is embodied more intensely in its thingness, in its being thing-like in a thingness that materializes in a tangible thing, and thus *the Real* is embodied not as a static thing but in its thing-like coming into being, just as the Israeli internal tensions are a network that embodies the real of anxiety. Therefore, trauma and denial-related tensions are responsible for creating the dream of this subjectivity. This same dream veils *the Real* even more intensely, veils the very fact that it is a dream.

There is also room for asking how this dream of Israeli subjectivity is organized along the axes of **time and temporality**.

Following Freud's *The Interpretation of Dreams*,[19] we may assume that even when the dream is conversing with the times of reality and with the times of *the Real* (the thing-like basis of the thing and of the reality that is inaccessible to us), the temporality of the dream is still different from that of the reality, namely, the being of time is different. And since an ideological, historical order is producing a dreaminess of Israeliness, it also establishes the temporality of the dream of Israeliness. This temporality is autonomous, and in its **puddle**, the dimension of anxiety does not necessarily refer to the temporal objects of reality. Anxiety refers to a super-temporal or a-temporal temporality (beyond the negation of temporality), while the past nothingness and the future nothingness are timeless beings.

And when there is a **translation** of the interior anxiety toward the levels of public discourse, then the real eternal object is translated into very temporal and concrete objects that blind both our eyes and our consciousness, objects which are a camouflage, not the thing itself but a translation of the Real.

The task of translation into the sexual, imaginary, and aggressive-competitive field (while skipping the impartial, logical symbolic in its purity) positions the thing and its **processive** thingness (processive within the dreamy Israeliness and not in reality) in a temporary-real temporality: here and now there is such and such an enemy in such and such military combat, in such and such terror attack.

In the **meta-psychic** sense, it may be said that the puddle founds the enemy in order to constantly orient the subject to the exterior time and to the concrete objects (but whose truth is not thing-like but imaginary). It is the imaginary temporality of beings in concrete reality.

Only in this way is it possible to comprehend how the imaginary-threatening beings are riding time spots in the past, present, and future. The puddle prevents its self-negation and recognition of nothingness through real objects moving toward it via the imaginary time axes:

The Nazi = from the past > to the present and future
The Arab = from the present > to the past and future
The Iranian = from the nuclear future > to the present

And so forth, in diverse and strange variations, the time axes enable the subject to imagine these beings not as camouflage to the nothing but as concrete objects of **concrete, real time**. And a redeemer shall come to Zion!

Though it may be pretentious to summarize our contentions thus far, which have been associated with those of Heidegger, Freud, and Lacan, in a sort of slight misreading to accommodate the concepts to the present state of affairs, we may still feel some of the thingness concerning which the Israeli anxiety is set in motion.

As we have attempted to show, the degree of anxiety, with its increasing expansion, may lead precisely to modes of foreclosure or **negation of the negation of the nothing**. It is an aporetic process that, contrary to the neurotic psychoanalytical position, does not necessarily produce dialectic repression but:

- A perverse denial while adopting the "enemy" object as a reconciliatory-sacred fetish (in the Freudian sense).[20]
- A psychotic act of effacing the dialectical negation without leaving a trace of being that is reminiscent of the nothing.[21]

In both cases, the being covering the nullification is eliminated, marked as an enemy being without any substitute. But the Israeliness also loses its anxiety and is being reborn as non-melancholic, non-occidental, non-Ashkenazi, and non-democratic, as these stereotypes these days tend to attach themselves to one another following the vehement right-wing discourse. In this discourse, the subjective interlocutor attempts to disengage him/herself from the mechanisms of psychic dialectics and from a neurotic internal speech, such as

> I fear the object 'Iran,' but I am not anxious because the object 'Iran' is not really threatening because I am strong but perhaps not that strong so I also repress this small thing so that I may have a joyful, peaceful life...

However, today joy is not a neutral factor. It is an unmistakable identifying signifier within a stereotypical equation between, on the one hand,

Ashkenazi, leftist, gay, western, democratic, cold, dead, melancholic, alienated, bureaucratic,

and, on the other hand:

Mizrahi, joyful, alive, rightist, nationalist, family-oriented, religious, observant, patriotic, liberated.

This is, of course, a very crude classification, a manipulative one, which today serves to strengthen the anti-democratic forces in Israel led by the king of Israel – Benyamin Netanyahu. The spirit of present times allows for it, and it is inevitably different from the heart that prevailed a decade or two ago. Today, Mizrahi music is suddenly light-hearted and happy when it was considered melancholic until not too long ago.

In this game of identifications, Netanyahu sets the tone by marking both the exterior enemy as well as the interior one who is even more ferocious, all the while continuing to produce new enemies, sounding the alarm of the Iranian threat, which is close, quite close, to the nullifying real we have discussed.

The word employed by Netanyahu to sum up the opposite axis of his camp is "pickles"[22] (employing a play of words between an active subject, which is sour, and the thing-like object, which is the pickled vegetable), the term he used in his infamous speech in the Israeli parliament. Previously, before the 1999 elections, he marked the interior enemy by stating "they a-r-e s-c-a-r-e-d" in some of his campaign speeches. He thus transferred from "they are scared" (vocally emphasizing the syllables with the intent to scare the scared) to "pickles" (perhaps while fermenting them – making them "sour"). The interior enemy is the one bearing the burden of anxiety or the "Ashkenazi," leftist melancholia, perhaps in confluence with the threatening thing, while the liberated, rightist, and Israeli subject is happy and content. The pickle is a colloquial signifier, Israeli – pleasurable as such, the user of which knows how to have fun, as opposed to the sour one. It is possible that at the unconscious level of the puddle, this signifier may interplay with another signifier – "aliens" (in Hebrew, "khutzanim," echoing "khamutzim").

Thus, the current Israeli anxiety is increasingly being translated into the instant political field and exploited for internal political gain, while continuously translating the inconceivable into concrete beings. The Israeli anxiety, which is one substance, subject-object, is being transformed into two separate substances:

anxiety<> Israeliness

Each of them is antagonistic to the other and does not even define itself through this antagonism but by virtue of indifference. This contrasts with our previous model:

anxiety = Israeliness

However, we must seriously consider that the manipulation, which is a deceitful course, will not necessarily impede a real Real. *Ultimately*, the real is attached to and is the outcome of *the Imaginary*, just as it is an outcome of *the Symbolic* (as a Möbius inversion). Therefore, the imaginary may produce a new real and erase the old one. Indeed, it is possible that all that has been argued in the present essay is but an error, for we are on the side of the "pickles."

It seems that the most genuine and the most horrid refuge behind the concealment is the fact that **there is no refuge behind the concealment at all**. This is unbearable and more oppressive than the very thought of refuge behind the concealment. Namely, contrary to the logic that we have presented, whereby the concealment conceals the fact that it covers, here the concealment hides the fact that there is nothing to conceal and that there is no concealment at all (all this following Heidegger's various formulations concerning the Greek concept of the truth about truth as *Aletheia* [disclosure]).[23]

If this is so, then the liberation from the loop of the theological-political thought of refuge behind the concealment toward a state of joy may produce a less horrific but nevertheless real. All this follows the monotheistic sense, whereby the proof for God's existence is established on the seemingly naïve stupidity of the transcendent non-presence of God, which translates into emergency anxiety, in the Schmidtian, explicitly fascist, sense.

The following is Netanyahu's "pickles" speech addressed to parliament members from the opposition. Some of the expressions may reflect many of the elements we have mentioned, for Netanyahu himself analyzes Israeli happiness vis-à-vis the great, ominous nothingness around us, threatened by enemies from both home and from afar:

> The industry of demoralization still exists and has honorable representatives in this very house [of parliament] and in the media. Recently, there is a renovation, a new branch has appeared – the pickles branch. [...] They used to grow etrogs, now they moved to pickles...It is hard for you, the pickles [...]
>
> In the most recent international ranking of happiness, the citizens of Israel ranked themselves in 5th place. Still, the young ones under the age of 29 rated themselves, pay attention pickles, in the 2nd place.
>
> The citizens of Israel know that life here is good. Israel is a beloved homeland, a warm home without a shred of cynicism, a formidable country. Israelis travel abroad in huge numbers – over 3 million Israelis have been abroad during the summer and the holidays. An incredible number. And upon returning, what do they say? And we hear this repeatedly, they say that there's no place like our country, no place like Israel; they see the revival, the levers, the buildings. We are turning Israel into a cyber, high-tech, intelligence, and water power.
>
> Let any enemy threatening to destroy us know that it risks mortal danger. At the same time, we extend our hand in peace to all our neighbors. We yearn for true peace, not a false reconciliation with forces that still aspire to drive us out of here.
>
> [...] We have power, but we are not power-stricken nor complacent. We are still facing significant challenges, both inside and outside of Israel, not least of which is the need to impede Iran from having a military foothold in Syria. We are working tirelessly to protect our borders and, if necessary, also beyond them. Concurrently, we are determined to prevent Iran from developing nuclear weapons intended for our destruction. If it hadn't been for our consistent, determined activity over the past years, Iran would have acquired nuclear weapons a long time ago.[24]

Notice the expression, "no place like Israel": how the discourse of fun rapidly slides into a discourse of horror. Notice how this expression progresses unconsciously toward a logic:

No place (=equals) like Israel

and to how the enemy is not futuristic but it is an annihilating force, as part of the following option:

Its being that had existed in an alternative future- present-time

but quite concrete.

Namely, there is an alteration of the fun and horror into **a different optional time**

and a different optional place,

an alternative future and an alternative vacationing country.

In light of the above speech, perhaps we are still touching upon a real that is impossible to shred, according to which **Israeliness = happiness**, is the *Das Ding* of the anxiety of Israeliness, undigestible happiness, the experience of which is felt only when multiplying our vacations abroad...

In doing so, we approach the kind of enjoyment that makes us stumble upon the thing and upon its thingness and what Lacan has coined as *jouissance*, which may be understood as follows: the thingness of enjoyment in its exaggeration is but uncontrollable, terrible suffering that entraps the subject while defining it in its unique specificity. Indeed, this is the exaggerated, unbearable enjoyment in our encounter with the *Das Ding*,[25] but its unbearableness, terribleness, or tremendousness camouflage its absence and its logical impossibility from the point of view of *the symbolic order*, which invents and at the same time nullifies it, and *the imaginary*, which furnishes it with transparent formats of "cultural" meaning.

Naturally, the problem does not arise unless one extremely specific side in the political map has the power to accord itself alone legitimacy to participate and have a voice in the political order, thus defining the interior essence of Israeliness, and its accompanying *jouissance*. Indirectly and unconsciously, this power is now the only power that defines and establishes the real of such essence by processing the symbolic and *imaginary*. It seems that it is possible to conceal or efface *the real*."

Notes

1 This essay has been previously translated into French by Avner Lahav and published in *La règle du jeu* (ed. Bernard-Henri Lévy), No. 68, 2019.
2 Heidegger, Martin, "Der Ursprung des Kunstwerkes", *Holzwege*, Frankfurt: Klostermann, 2003. See also, Heidegger, Martin, "The Thing", *Bremen and Freiburg Lectures*, trans. Andrew J. Mitchell, Bloomington, Indiana: Indiana University Press, 2012, p. 5.
3 Freud, Sigmund, "Project for a Scientific Psychology", in *The Origins of Psycho-Analysis: Letters to Wilhelm Fliess, Drafts and Notes: 1887–1902*, transl. J. Strachey et al., New York: Basic Books, 1954, pp. 347–445. https://doi.org/10.1037/11538-013. (1895), *GW Nacht.*: 375–486.
4 Lacan, Jacques, *The Seminar of Jacques Lacan, Book VII: The Ethics of Psychoanalysis, 1959–1960*, ed. J.A. Miller, trans. Denis Porter, London and New York: Routledge, 1999.

5 Gadamer, Hans-Georg, *Truth and Method*. 2nd rev. edition, transl. J. Weinsheimer and D. G. Marshall, New York: Crossroad, 2004, pp. 268–278.
6 Heidegger, Martin, *On the Way to Language*. ed. 1st Harper & Row pbk., San Francisco: Harper San Francisco, 1982.
7 Lacan, Jacques, *The Seminar of Jacques Lacan, Book X: Anxiety*, ed. J. A. Miller, Polity Books, 2014.
8 Lacan, Jacques, *Écrits: The First Complete Edition in English*, transl. Bruce Fink, New York: W.W. Norton & Company, 2006, pp. 413–414.
9 Lacan, Jacques, *Écrits: The First Complete Edition in English*, transl. Bruce Fink, New York: W.W. Norton & Company, 2006, pp. 413–414.
10 Derrida, Jacques, *The Gift of Death*, trans. D. Wills, Chicago: University of Chicago Press, 1966.
11 Freud, Sigmund, "Inhibition, Symptom and Anxiety", *The Standard Edition of the Complete Psychological Works of Sigmund Freud*, trans. James Stratchy, 20, 1926, pp. 75–176.
12 Freud, Sigmund, "Inhibition, Symptom and Anxiety", *The Standard Edition of the Complete Psychological Works of Sigmund Freud*, trans. James Stratchy, 20, 1926, pp. 75–176.
13 Jacques Lacan, *Anxiety*.
14 Heidegger, Martin, *Pathmarks*, ed. W. McNeill, Cambridge: Cambridge University Press, 1998, p. 88.
15 Lacan, Jacques, *The Seminar of Jacques Lacan, Book 1: Freud's Papers on Technique, 1953–1954*, ed. Jacques Alain Miller, transl. John Forrester, New York: W.W. Norton & Company, 1991.
16 Freud, Sigmund, "The Uncanny", *The Standard Edition of the Complete Psychological Works of Sigmund Freud, Volume XVII (1917–1919): An Infantile Neurosis and Other Works*, transl. A. Stratchy, London: Hogarth, 1925, p. 226.
17 Lacan, Jacques, *The Seminar of Jacques Lacan: Book XI: The Four Fundamental Concepts of Psychoanalysis*, ed. J.-A. Miller, transl. A. Sheridan, New York: W.W Norton, 1978, p. 156.
18 Lacan, Jacques, *The Seminar of Jacques Lacan: Book XI: The Four Fundamental Concepts of Psychoanalysis*, ed. J.-A. Miller, transl. A. Sheridan, New York: W.W Norton, 1978, p. 156, pp. 53–58.
19 Freud, Sigmund, *The Interpretation of Dreams*, transl. J. Crick, Oxford: Oxford University Press, 1999.
20 Sigmund Freud, "Fetishism", *International Journal of Psychoanalysis 9*, transl. Joan Riviere, 1928, pp. 161–166.
21 Lacan, Jacques, *The Seminar of Jacques Lacan: The Psychoses (1955–1956) – Book III*, ed. Jacques Alain Miller, transl. R. Grigg, New York: WW Norton & Co, 1977.
22 [The Hebrew word for "pickle" is the same word in Hebrew for "sour", or in plural "sours" (Hamutzim)].
23 Heidegger, Martin, *Pathmarks*, ed. W. McNeill, Cambridge: Cambridge University Press, 1998, p. 88.
24 Benyamin Netanyahu's speech in the Israeli parliament (the Knesset), *YouTube*: https://www.youtube.com/watch?v=yigG-NCDtog&ab_channel=Benjamin Netanyahu-%D7%91%D7%A0%D7%99%D7%9E% D7%99%D7%9F%D7% A0%D7%AA%D7%A0%D7%99%D7%94%D7%95, (October 23, 1917).
25 Lacan, Jacques, *The Seminar of Jacques Lacan: The Ethics of Psychoanalysis – Book VII*, ed. J- A Miller, transl. D. Porter, New York: WW Norton & Co, 1997.

Chapter 5

There Is Something of the Mizrahiness

On Re-Inscribing Identity Contents Retrospectively

An identifying axis is stirring the dynamics of Israel's perpetual acute political crisis. It may seem like a political crisis of sovereignty, but its semi-concealed aspect points to a profound social problem. The axis that perpetuates this insolvability convolutes within this dynamic as it is afflicted with modes of reference to the word "Mizrahiness" and the current identity of this identifying signifier.[1]

This crisis is so all-inclusive that this *political* does not give room for almost any other *political*. It exists under a imaginary fabric, which is seemingly fictitious but quite effective, and, as such, reinscribes all other modes of the *political* as fantasy. We diagnose this crisis under the signifier *Mizrahiness*, with all its biases. In contrast, the material and structural aspects of this signifier, seemingly empty and devoid of significance, are already located in a phantasmatic political space that tints it from its inception with various significations on which the polemics brush against the totality of problems that define and rip apart the Israeli society.

The hermeneutical twists and turns voiced by the ministers in the market and government merchants and invested in the word *Mizrahiness* engender it with internal conversions, be it in channeling the tensions or explaining the structure of the intra-Israeli tensions between the right and the left wings, the religious and the seculars, Zionists, and anti-Zionists, and even between Arabs and Jews. Consequently, those who are willingly or unwillingly defined as *Mizrahi* are condensed in a verbal compound that compresses the totality of the intra-Israeli tensions into a single conceptual space.

If this is so, we could inquire how an intra-linguistic dynamic concerning the word *Mizrahiness* echoes the internal political dynamics and is echoed within it, thereby allowing the question of how this word reflects the various histories of the intra-Israeli tensions. The hermeneutics of the term *Mizrahi* calls for a discussion on the relationship between the way we perceive it in the present and its historical sense found professedly in the past and the various origins of the word.

***

DOI: 10.4324/9781003667339-5

It seems impossible to conduct a political discussion on *Mizrahiness* without examining its mode of definition, even more than its content. Our mission is to explore the logic behind the definition of *Mizrahiness* as an idiosyncratic cultural-communal space as a prerequisite to the inquiry of the political implications of this definition as reflected in the political metaphysics; for example, as reflected in the right-wing politics whose conspicuous representative is Avishay Ben-Haim.[2]

I shall attempt to show that the presence of the signifier *Mizrahiness* exists within an identificational-mythical circularity which in Lacanian terms constitutes a *quilting point* (*point de capiton*) for the various contents of various agents across the political, cultural, and academic spheres, as well as the personal and familial ones, including salon conversations among family members, and the discussion of the self with its selfhood, be it a Mizrahi selfhood or otherwise.

Social contents, political positions, modes of cultural identification, as well as of choosing and voting, are infiltrated into this obnubilated signification of meaning. Notwithstanding, this chapter wishes to prove that it is impossible to distinguish between plain manipulation and dignifying intent. It perceives the all-encompassing ideological space as one that continuously reinscribes historical meanings of signifiers, in this case, the signifier *Mizrahi*. Thereby, the ideological space is generating its own subjects.

For example, we may perceive the ideological procedure serving Netanyahu's right as a tautological logic constructed as a closed circle, following Ben-Haim's unidirectional formulation: *Mizrahiness* is defined through the prism of supporting Netanyahu, and the support of Netanyahu is expressed through the prism of *Mizrahiness*.[3]

Thus, the definition of *Mizrahiness* is not one pertaining to content but one related to structure: it unwittingly places *Mizrahiness* under the tautological structuring of the bidirectional relation to Netanyahu. It is indeed a bidirectional tautology that reduces *Mizrahiness* to a single dimension whose purpose is one: to vote for Netanyahu. But in fact, this procedure is no different than any other tendencies attempting to define *Mizrahiness*, from the political and social reductions of the emancipatory left-wing to the cultural and postcolonial reductions; while they may have bestowed an element of content on the definition of *Mizrahiness*, they remain subordinated to the structural mode of adding meaning, which is forever mythical, phantasmatical, and partial. Such is the case with the following definition: while it may seem that we have a substantial definition that implies that the Mizrahiness, as the ultimate representative of the "Second Israel," considers Netanyahu its subversive savior, this is, in fact, merely a structural definition, for it enchains *Mizrahiness* to the one who is perceived as its sole representative. Thus, it has to do with the position of the signifier *Mizrahi*.

The presence of the signifier, rather than its meaning, is embodied in the fact that many Israelis have a premonition regarding the supposedly authentic

Mizrahiness, while the use of the linguistic signifier is the central axis of this premonition. Let us begin at the end, where we already have a postulate regarding Mizrahiness, which will provide an anchor for our retrospective. But this is a signifying anchor. When we say, "there is something of the *Mizrahiness*," we first and foremost say, "there is something of the signifier '*Mizrahi*,'" and only then do we assume its contents. By this, we unwittingly assume a relationship between "there is Mizrahiness" as a signifier and "there is something of," which is the product of guessing the content of "there is *Mizrahiness*." This relationship between the definitive postulate regarding the signifier and the speculation regarding the signified is the structurality that enables the retrospective running around and about, which we will attempt to describe as follows.

***

Because our concern here is with the *current* intuition, the only standpoint at hand for explaining *Mizrahiness* is the one we currently possess in the present. As appropriate to retrospective thinking, one can only respond from the current perspective in the theoretical prism of the retroactive. Namely, from the standpoint of the presentness and the authenticity of the *Mizrahiness*, we must examine the timeline folded within it. In compliance with the Freudian concept, *Nachträglichkeit* (literally: what comes afterward, belatedness), I propose the following scheme regarding the three stages of the fantasy. We use the three stages with some flexibility that may guide us through the current discussion:

1 A forgotten (possibly) real event that occurred in the distant past.
2 An event remembered from the present past or from the conscious past-present.
3 The present existence.

```
-------------→
←------
1-----2-----3
```

Event 2 inscribes for the present existence 3 the first concrete event 1 as genuine and actual, albeit phantasmatic or tinted as such in light of the second event 2 remembered by the present existence 3. Thus, to a certain extent, the very subject existing in the present in the flesh is born retrospectively out of receptacle 1. This may sound odd as this receptacle is born out of an occurrence experienced by 3 under his/her present existence 2. Hence, subjectivity is the space of the phantasm that remembers a past currently existing in the present, and is even more present than the present itself, as it is perceived as original and primal. This teaches us that the subject denies the self-manipulation of the presentness, him/her being merely a derivative of the distress of the present, while the entire past is no more than a story of the present, rather than the kernel of existence. In this sense, the unconscious that seems like a motion from the past toward the present is merely the motion from the present toward the past, and the revealing of the repressed is not one of unveiling the past but of exposing the present in light of a past inscribed via the present. Let us proceed with this insight to thinking about identification or mythology of identity, specifically (the mythology of) *Mizrahiness*.

This is not to say that there is not something of the Mizrahim, nor that the Mizrahi sociocultural phenomenon is null. We shall attempt to indicate these substances as expressing a mythical structure or as stemming from one that continuously engenders a specific ad hoc instantaneous identity for itself. For us, this identity is intimately connected to the present experience, to our needs, *hic et nunc*. But from this point onward, being entirely wrought from the raw material of the signifier, this structure rereads the entire identificational space within a complex topological structure while smashing truths and lies and diffusing them by continually slamming them against each other.

We are all trapped in this mythical circle, beginning with "Ashkenazi" or "Mizrahi" and continuing with intellectuals, people of culture, academics, and more. According to this formulation, identity is trapped in an ontological structure, which may be demonstrated as that mythical circle in which human existence is usually trapped. This mythical circle both traps and holds every human activity, be it a partial activity perceived by itself as progressive, liberated, conservative, or reactionary. Within this circle, existence is inscribed under the impression of empty signifiers that do not "really" carry any stable meaning but are inscribed in an odd topological circle between the past and the present. In contrast, this circle impinges upon a more advanced one of past–present–future, albeit imaginary.

In this circle, past events are inscribed as founding the subject's existence in the present – be it the subject as the bearer of the caption "Mizrahi" or the assigner of this signifier to others. The keyword here seems to be "inscribed"; an event is inscribed as such when it is engraved in our flesh for various reasons, often unknown to us. Its inscription in the subject's flesh occurs most likely retrospectively, not from the past to the present but from the present or an immediate past towards a more distant one. The inscription rends the question "did it happen or not" superfluous, meaning whether or not the event "really" occurred is irrelevant in this context, for the specific inscription of the event in the subject's history – the inscription that forms a history for the subject – is what constitutes the event as a mental fact, which is at the same time ontological, ontological subjectivity. The inscription traverses the dichotomies of objectivity/subjectivity and ontology/epistemology: it constitutes a mental fact. The wonder of this retroactive motion is that there is absolutely no objective past lying behind the present, contrary to common sense. The past is added retrospectively to the present as what constitutes the present. Namely, the present, allegedly founded by the past, founds the past, appointing it as its own founder of the present.

Suppose we return to the mythical circle in which we are all trapped. In that case, the empty signifier of sense and identity proves to be the present's current point of departure via which we retroactively reread the past. As aforesaid, this is not a mere epistemological issue regarding the mode of perceiving the past, but indeed a reconstitution of the past in a manner that inscribes our existence in the present time. Thus, the present inscribes the past that inscribes our present: this infers that the present inscribes itself to suit a certain interest, mostly related to materiality, acclaim, or power. This does not imply a simple act of deception but rather one that engenders history, identity, and certainty.

The origin of *Mizrahiness* is inscribed as such only in retrospection, by way of the retroactive motion of *Mizrahiness* from its present embodiments that register its history in reverse. That is, here, 2 is not a past event but an aspect of the present. If we look at history in reverse, following Walter Benjamin's "angel of history," then we shall discover two principal "origins" that would not be found in the past in a primal-clean way but first and foremost in the present, as vibrant vitality, the present reproducing the origin retroactively.

The first "origin" is the Arabic, in a crease of identification denial; I feel Arabic within, live as an Arab culturally, but detest the Arab externally so that I may distinguish myself from the enemy of Zionism and solidify my status within the identificational discomfort and inferiority within the Zionist-Ashkenazi space. This structure does not argue for a belated recognition of the "Arabic" at the basis of *Mizrahiness* or retrospective self-knowledge, nor that denial of the Arabic is a belated reconstruction of solid historical truth, albeit denied, must be fully uncovered. Instead, it argues that the present inscribes the past of the Arabic, literally creating the past, which now creates the present. Even then, this scheme is being written in its entirety in the present.

Denial does not imply a false or worthless position. It is a concrete existential being in which the logic of abjection is inscribed; the abject (the Arabic), the internal–external (Arab Jew), is inscribed as entirely external to preserve the "internal" (Jew, or *Mizrahi* Jew, the latter being an Arab Jew minus the Arab). The denial of the identification with the Arab is the origin. Therefore, there is something of the *Mizrahiness* is the origin of this present. And this present retroactively inscribes the history of the Jews together with that of the Arabs. This is the anchor of the ideology.

The second "origin" is the space of the synagogue, in which many immigrants from Islamic countries together formed a religious space, which is understood today as traditional, a physical space reminiscent of a members' club that provides a sense of community, neighborhood, commonality of knowledge, and mentality. This present origin is even more significant, for it is not denied, nor does it exclude other Jews who are not necessarily from Arab countries, such as immigrants from Iran or India. In the chaos of the synagogue that has already lost the various origins of its diverse communities, is there any sense in reconstructing a past origin when the present existence alone inscribes the historical? Or is it that there might be a point in doing so, but mustn't we acknowledge that this reconstruction also involves a constitution and not just disclosure and exposure?

The present existence is an undeniable origin: there *is* something of traditionalism. And the orthodoxy put in place by the *Shas* party,[4] which the writer of this chapter also has considered until recently an enemy of the Mizrahi traditionalism, may be understood within this theoretical context as one that retrospectively invented traditionalism as a moderate religious position rather than ultra-orthodox or even counter-Ashkenazi (via its theo-political slogan, "to restore past glory").[5] We cannot underrate the value of origin and authenticity of the phenomenon of traditionalism. The traditional subject experiences traditionalism as authentic and primal, even if it is not authentic but founded within a complex topology of past–present constitutional relationships.

Furthermore, a double origin of denial of identification with the Arabic and with the Mizrahi traditionalism has recently attained a political present organization. Is this political reduction a stifling one? Or does it, following our analysis, inscribe *Mizrahiness* similarly to its other inscriptions? While we could identify the previous original present as authentic from its present perspective, is there now a unilateral translation of this present into the space of party politics? We may argue that this reduction shapes *Mizrahiness* as supporting Netanyahu and that the Likud party reproduces the Mizrahiness, distorting its present origins and all its characteristics, for example, praying, food, etc., or place of residence. But the suggested topology does not effectuate a simple response to the enigma of this ideology of identity, for the Mizrahi *identity* is allegedly distorted by its very definition.

Since the Likud party came to power, there has been a reduction of the *Mizrahiness* to a political ethnonational conception, which, even if it possesses some current solidification, is not essential to the extra-political existence. Is this true or false? Or does the nature of opacity account for this political phylogenesis? And yet, how may we explain the way in which this "Likudism" is not a present origin but merely a manipulative one? Does a present origin nevertheless need to refer to some past origin, even if it is a transformational phantasmatic past? For Freud, it does not mean that the phantasmatic primary event 2 did not originate in a real event 1. There *was* something, but it has been (re)written.

Do the politicization and the nationalization of *Mizrahiness* and traditionalism during the last decades, which serve certain factors in the nationalist right-wing (or pseudo-nationalist *a la* Netanyahu), have nothing in common with the present phantasmatic origins of the *Mizrahiness*, of the "something of the *Mizrahiness*"? Or do they have an affinity to these origins because these right-wing factors are part and parcel of the constant construction of its reinvented past and present identities that look upon the past and even the future – suggesting that they do bear something of the *Mizrahiness* (and here perhaps we must part with the position of the Mizrahi left and its argument that

Mizrahiness is essentially – or by virtue of its history – moderate, soothed, and reconciling Islam with Judaism, rather than divisive and violent as is the European thought and existence)?

***

And what about the institutional oppression of the Mizrahim? Was there no oppression in the past? Is there none in the present?

It must be recognized that topologically the actual oppression cannot be isolated from identifying the oppression of the very signifier of Mizrahiness; that is, the oppression is invented retroactively, vested by a factor that is perceived as unified and monolithic and directed within a straightforward narrative such as the state or the Ashkenazi or some other master concerning the Mizrahi as a monolithic factor shaped in the present. This present shapes the past as oppression and the master as oppressor in a way that, in turn, reshapes the Mizrahi in the present. But the fact that the Mizrahi identity is constituted retroactively does not mean that there was no oppression.

If we follow the logic of inscription, the oppression occurred because it has been inscribed, and not just in individual experiences but also as a social phantasm beyond the categories of truth or lie or reality or myth: as a phantasmatic ontology, so to speak, which is part and parcel of the Mizrahi identity. Moreover, the moment of trauma bears significance in the retroactive dynamics of the continuous engendering of the sense of victimization based on a past present that engenders the current present and the past. Furthermore, the element of victimization or trauma cannot characterize the engendering essence of the *Mizrahiness*, as these are historical aspects or constructed as such, which may be applied to any community. Therefore, victimization, weakness, or oppression are not idiosyncratic to the Mizrahi, but they safely position it as a mediating factor among the multiplicity of other components in the Israeli society, given that the Israeli identity is constructed from a succession of identities, each one solidifying its identity through being a victim, in one way or another.

Victimization is both an asset and a weapon within the Israeli internal power struggles. While the position of the victim does not define identity in essence, it serves as a formative or empowering factor within the intricate dynamics between victimization and democratic existence, while the expressed aim of the liberal democracy is to protect the underprivileged minorities, which are so very often actively excluded.

Despite the tangibility of oppression and its implications, such as geographic and cultural peripherality, they cannot be disconnected from their being organized by the present point of view. According to Freud's position regarding trauma, it is possible that a constitutive event was inscribed in the subject's mind, but from the very beginning, it was inscribed as constitutive in the phantasmatic space. The memory of the event dwells within the phantasmatic space of the present or another, more recent event that inscribes it retrospectively as traumatic. Thus, the myth of the Mizrahiness, and the traumatic nature attached to it, may comprise those who are referred to today as "Mizrahim," whether they had been institutionally oppressed in the past or not, or had not been aware of the past oppression but today inscribe and experience it retrospectively.

Oppression, education tracking, and discrimination, which all existed in the past and still exist, have been directed toward various communities, not necessarily under the dialectical tension of a pronounced master and a pronounced slave. This has to do with the narcissistic and present aspect of mythology or fantasy. This oppression was directed toward me as a Mizrahi, both in the past and present. I see myself not oppressed in general in the past, but oppressed as Mizrahi. This identification reshapes the past retrospectively, founding my monolithic identity under the signifier Mizrahi. It is an identificational magic circle that constantly reinforces my identity as Mizrahi, precisely in an era when communal identities are presumed to collapse for economic, cultural, political, personal reasons, and more.

***

One may argue that the current politicization of Mizrahiness is the outcome of a strategy that employs characteristics associated with the daily existence of those identified as Mizrahi – the food, the language, the residential place, the memories, the prayer – generating a manipulation that emphasizes, empowers, and even distorts such characteristics, containing them under the signifier "Mizrahi." In this context, one may refer to Marxist terminology of alienation, or *Entfremdung*, the distancing of the self from its selfhood, as alienation from the most basic human condition, *Gattungswesen*, resulting in an ideological manipulation and political exploitation of one social group or another. Hence, the self-political alienation no longer enables a dialectic between present and past, which is the living substance of the term "Mizrahi," and, in this manner, annihilates it from within. Are we left with a word that has only an external vitality, with a dead – or deadened – interiority?

If so, this interior death enables the continuity of the economic and cultural oppressions of the Mizrahi, even if it seems that this very Mizrahiness has won over the Israeli culture and is omnipresent. The Israeli space has embraced the Mizrahi attributes (with or without inverted commas) and assimilated them – from the Kebab to the Mizrahi music – so that today there are no longer cultural aspects that are unique to Mizrahi. Henceforth, we may even contend that what has remained exclusively Mizrahi has been effaced, purified from within, and turned into a political space of maneuvers that serves the interests of other segments of the population, such as the monopolists on the one hand, and the settlers in the occupied territories, on the other.

In this light, we may also examine the Mizrahi supporters of Netanyahu: away from the sociological question of whether most Mizrahim indeed support Netanyahu, we are required to ponder upon the very question, that is, upon the exact link between Mizrahim and the support of Netanyahu. This link has generated a political entanglement not easily escapable, for it has retrospectively reinscribed Mizrahiness as retroactive support of Netanyahu. At the same time, the past reinforces the current Mizrahi identity as supporting Netanyahu.

***

From the perspective of the real, there is an instance where all the signifiers seem void and, as such, are reinscribed by all the various categories with no exception: democracy, Judaism, Israelism, and Mizrahiness. The signifier "Mizrahiness" here bears an ontological surplus rather than ontological preference[6]: it is a super-signifier that captures the network of all other signifiers, for it captures together all the shortcomings of Israeli existence. Let us further zero in on this issue by pointing to the particularity of the signifier "Mizrahi":

a   The context of oppression and trauma proclaims the signifier "Mizrahi" as signifying the repressed within or controlled by order of the master, it being the sole preoccupation of the master in relation to the slave (thus, e.g., the signifier "Mizrahi," in its prior reincarnations as well, bears in the internal Israeli context a negative or derogatory charge, similar to the one borne by the *Ostjuden*, the east-European Jew, at the time).
b   The concept is controversial and demands constant discussion regarding its historical accuracy and relevance to political discourse in a controversial turmoil that, by its very existence, accentuates the presence and relevance of this signification in relation to the political field.

Because this signifier complies with both conditions, we may assume that it does not refer to the positive sociocultural content that it purports to describe and that many people carry it as an ornament or a heavy burden. As we have seen, this is not a conceptual content but rather a signifying presence pertaining to the very sound of the utterance "Mizrahi." The chain of signification evolves from a present that charges the term and turns it into the concept, reshaping past meanings, and from the past reverberates to the present, charging it with seemingly positive content. This magic circle endows the empty signifier with vitality and a quasi-real presence.

Avishay Ben-Haim perceives the Mizrahim as a traditional Jewish collective who immigrated from Islamic countries, whose mentality does not fully correspond to the western rationale, even though they participate in the Western Israeli Zionist project of emancipation and have suffered and still suffer from oppression and discrimination by the Ashkenazi collective, which denied them the realization of their professional, personal, cultural, and housing aspirations. Without the intent to endorse any political tendency, I argue that Ben-Haim's claim may be seen as an example of this back-and-forth motion discussed above, in which the signifier is charged in the present with meanings that retroactively inscribe it in a way that again reshapes current identity and so forth. Particularly, Mizrahim, who aspire to break through the boundaries of their prior assigned space, suffer from legal, bureaucratic, "rational," and "Ashkenazi" violence aimed to obstruct them. This legal violence may materialize both against concrete Mizrahi representatives and, as Ben-Haim claims to have learned from Antonio Gramsci and his followers, against a populist leader – Netanyahu – whom the Mizrahi representatives use in order to attack the Ashkenazi oppressive elite. Hence, when Netanyahu serves as a means to the Mizrahi project of liberation, Ben-Haim reinscribes Mizrahiness in Israeli politics.

Hopefully, this theoretical endeavor may provide some relief from the bafflement involved in the difficulty of refusing the temptation to assume a critical position. Perhaps at this point, we may position the right-wing *a la* Netanyahu, without justifying it, within the wide mythologization of Mizrahiness, or any other identity for that matter. This positioning does not imply the annihilation of the political space but rather a deeper insight into the difficulty of confronting the entanglement between identity and the political.

***

Concerning the difficulty of refusing the temptation of assuming a critical position toward the Mizrahi right-wing, there are voices in the Mizrahi left-wing oriented avant-garde intelligence, which attempt to extricate the Mizrahiness from this seemingly exploitative rhetoric, at times consciously and at times in denial of the fact that this avant-garde is itself a derivative of that same ideological dynamic of retroactivity. This dynamic also bears the moment of liberation in this instance, but it cannot liberate *itself* from its foundational mythological circularity. The Mizrahi politics of freedom is not cut off from the phantasmatic assumptions and constructions that define it either, again, phantasmatically, as a politics of liberation.

In effect, that same Mizrahi avant-garde cannot recognize that it is, among other things, both *the* object of that same retroactive mythology and the product of this dynamic that perceives Mizrahiness as a liberating space. The very thought of this liberation is the product of ideological dynamics whose aim is to create a consciousness that tells itself the story of Mizrahiness as the origin that suffered in the past under a real event in the "Maabarot"[7] and is presently suffering under what is termed as the "First Israel," free of manipulation or inscription via the present. The Mizrahi intellectual is the invention *par excellence* of the same logic, an invention that cannot speak out against itself. To put it another way, the Mizrahi intellectual who aspires to liberation incarnates the very structure of *Nachträglichkeit* unless he/she is willing to recognize this menacing fact.

Therefore, for those seeking an authentic Mizrahiness, it may help to suggest the following aporia: because Mizrahiness is an invented identity, particularly by the state and the elite, those who adopt it literally, as the product of the other's gaze upon them, are precisely structurally inauthentic Mizrahim. In contrast, those adopting a critical, ironic distance from that Mizrahiness, a slight alienation which is construed ever so often as "becoming Ashkenazi," who recognize the inventiveness of the Mizrahiness, with a subtle differentiation from the Mizrahiness itself, are not necessarily more authentic but are perhaps less self-deceptive regarding their Mizrahi origin.

The Mizrahiness that adopts the Ashkenazi identity is a mythical identity, just like all other fictitious identities. Still, it reinscribes in retrospect both the Ashkenazi and the Mizrahi myths, producing a potentially liberating linking loop, for it points to the intrinsic structure of the Mizrahi identity itself. Therefore, one may suggest that the Mizrahi adopting the Ashkenazi identity is precisely the authentic Mizrahi, for she/he is at peace with her/his very structural relation to her/himself, whereas the one supposedly free from Ashkenaziness (which is, of course, itself an invention) is structurally in a constant state of alienation from his/her selfhood. The Mizrahi who relates to him/her/self of his/her authenticity is in denial of the past-present or present-past constant constitutive moment of his/her identity.

In this respect, the latter Mizrahi is not chained to a teleological finality but to an ironic, internal–external position that reads the chain of Mizrahiness retroactively, a reading that includes the other's gaze. The latter bearing something of the Other. The Other Mizrahi.

Notes

1 The literal meaning of the Hebrew "Mizrahi" is Oriental, as well as Eastern. Notwithstanding, in the discourse of Israeli immigration history and culture, it has come to designate all the immigrants (Olim Hadashim), whose countries of origin are in the Middle East and/or North Africa, also known as the Maghreb. The chapter refers to its signifying connotations. I have decided to keep the Hebrew term, in order not to confuse the specific attributions of the Hebrew "Mizrahi" with connotations and associations of the English equivalents.

2 Ben-Haim is an Israeli journalist, reporter, and researcher, whose work focuses on the Israeli orthodox and ultra-orthodox communities; he is a supporter of Netanyahu.

3 The majority of the Mizrahi population in Israel has been historically voting for right-wing parties, religious or secular (mainly for the Likud, the party led by Netanyahu for the last 15 years).

4 "Shas" (in Hebrew, ש"ס) was founded as a Mizrahi ultra-orthodox political party in 1984, by former Sephardi Chief Rabbi Ovadia Yosef who remained its spiritual leader until his death in 2013. As such, it represents mainly the interests of the Sephardic and Mizrahi ultra-orthodox Jews. But some secular and even left-wing Mizrahim have been known to vote for it, not because they identify with its political platform but because of the profound hatred and anger toward the Israeli left which is historically perceived as "Ashkenazi" and elitist.

5 Shas' original slogan during its political campaign.

6 Surplus in Hebrew = "odfut" (עודפות); preference = "adifut" (עדיפות), terms that reverberate each other.

7 Israeli immigrant and refugee transit-camps, populated in the 1950s, mostly by immigrant Jews from Islamic, north-African countries.

Chapter 6

The Political Ontology of Time

On Monday, July 24, 2023, at 15:43, our Israel was proclaimed dead. With a majority of 64 votes of the coalition members against 0 from the opposition, the parliament was granted a large portion of its "judicial reform"[1] cake, the enactment to abolish the legal norm of "reasonableness." We, as citizens, are now much lesser citizens. In what is to come, we will be less and less protected, as the sovereign grows stronger and stronger and more and more fortified. The State's fortress has fallen.

The big question ahead of us is whether we too will fall. Will we sink in despair or rather engage in a fierce struggle involving much sweat and perhaps another kind of fluid of the color red? What now? In what direction to lead the shame, the anger, the frustration, the despair, and the unreasonable hope? Shall we abandon the protest, abandon the country, or fight tooth and nail, fight in every corner, submit every possible petition to the High Court of Justice, abolish the abolishment of reasonableness, and restore reason to the country?

In writing these lines, I am attempting to take a deep breath through the stifling sense of pain and distress engulfing us to submerge myself in thought, so that I may make some sense of the entangled situation in which we are all submersed, to understand how to proceed from the moment of breakdown and whether there exists a strategic point thereafter. Do we have enough time? In this critical moment, Israel marks six months of forceful protestation against the judicial reform brought about by Benyamin Netanyahu and his government, purporting to put an end to its already vulnerable democratic system. The feelings in the streets of protestation oscillate between patriotic euphoria and anxious despair, between feelings of mourning and melancholy for having lost our country, and faith that from the crisis a new Israel might reemerge, notwithstanding all the "scientific" predictions regarding the demographic growth of anti-democratic groups.

Albeit a specific experience in time and place, this is related to and impacted by other resistance movements in the world battling with the threat of populist nationalistic movements that rush the political system to the collapse of the Rule of Law and of the parliamentary democratic system. It happened in Poland and in Hungary. In the United States, it almost happened with Trump,

DOI: 10.4324/9781003667339-6

and it might happen again, and will perhaps affect other countries in the West, such as France, the Netherlands, and Finland, which are traditionally perceived as strongholds of democracy and progress. As I aim to show, the consideration of the protestation along its temporal axis is pivotal to the understanding of its success or failure.

Since the inception of the resistance movement, the self-confidence and determination of its members have progressively increased, enabling them to take bolder actions – perhaps the result of this unparalleled blend of hope and despair – when it became clear that the government's prompt and devious response was to abolish the legal norm of reasonableness. But this is not a linear progression. Beyond its emotional turbulence, the movement is ultimately pondering on its very essence and purpose; its leaders, as well as each one of its members, incessantly and justly wondering what will be the ultimate effect?! Does our effort, heroic as it may be, bear any fruit? Could we impede the "judicial reform" against all odds, even after such a crucial moment? Perhaps here we should sharpen the question whether decided hopes colliding with deep despair, constituting a senseless vortex, are but a momentary unrest caused by circumstances, or rather, the two emotional tendencies produce a dialectical relation between them, namely a relation of mutual constitution and incitement? Is this about mere emotional tension, or does it also involve the state of the world and the nature of time from a philosophical perspective? Is it a question of perspective in relation to a given reality? Ultimately, the protesters are facing a wall, which is their harsh reality. A wall of unreasonableness.

Protesters are facing this wall at the same time as they are forced to grapple with brutal restraining means on the part of the police. Within a few month pause from the declaration to enact the judicial reform, which constitutes in fact an effacement, it was resumed more forcefully, galloping forward, physically and metaphorically, trampling over the State's body as it will shortly trample over the bodies of its concerned citizens, removing every obstacle from its path, disregarding the cries to pause if only for a moment to listen to the voice of the people, even if this voice belongs to half of the people, a deeply concerned half.

The force of this frustrating situation may easily tempt us to plunge into the pitfall of despair, for even though it has proved successful in restraining the course of the judicial reform to a certain degree, the protesters gradually realize that the other side is no less determined and obstinate, as attested by the voting today. From the cynical perspective of the other side, it is best to regulate the temporal pace, during which, on the one hand, the protestation in not fueled by too drastic measures, and on the other, the reform is positively catalyzed toward its final static stage, whereby the very right to protest will have been banned, which will permit these revolutionary reactionary forces to rest on the laurels of their everlasting government with no opposition whatsoever. Is this not a magic circle of determination and despair, within which both sides are caught in their pursuit of their temporal pace directed toward the decisive moment? Namely, the dilemma on both sides is how to organize what may be termed "time elasticity," rather than objective time, time as a dimension in which the action reverses the modes of temporal effectiveness onto the action itself. To some extent, the victorious side will be the one to have managed the temporal strategy more effectively. Perhaps, the vast march to Jerusalem that took place a few days prior to the parliament's act of abolishing reasonableness was too connected to this temporal regulation, for the marching itself is proclaiming that we will march and not stop before we tilt the balance; moreover, time is no longer managed by the government to target the parliament enactment, but is the time of the march targeting the moment that will generate change due to its own regulation of the temporal axis? The protest that is about to take place in Jerusalem following the parliament's voting, will be declaring by its very action that time is not owned solely by the rival and that what has been decided is not final; it is possible to turn back its wheels, to modify it, and to prevent the occurrence from becoming final and absolute.

All this is the response to the other side changing its strategy, following the Blitz address of the Minister of Justice, Yariv Levin, on January 4, 2023, presenting the judicial reform, merely six days from the swearing in of Netanyahu's new government. In view of the poignant response of the resistance, which took both its members as well as the opposition leaders (in the parliament) – being the rather impotent creatures that they are, whether men or women – by surprise, the Blitzkrieg strategy was replaced by the salami one, namely to advance the cause slowly but surely, slice by slice. But the timing is amiss. It is too late. It has become evident that this is but another, even dirtier ploy on the part of the government, which has induced much disbelief in it, even in the hearts of some past supporters. Even if some change in the judicial system is warranted, every future step taken by the government will be henceforth perceived as a step in the gamut of destroying democracy. So, both sides are caught in a determinism targeting a specific moment, navigating their actions, which they both chase or are chased by.

Furthermore, despite the burning desire to protect the democratic pact between the State and its people, and despite the determination to fight along the same dreadful temporal axis, one may sense that in relation to the progression of the judicial reform, a small doubt is whispering in the protesters' ears, "we have sacrificed long days protesting against their laws of dictatorship, what is the point now?"

The answer lies in the very question, notably in the word "now." The struggle for and against the reform in Israel is a struggle to reformat the temporal space: on the part of the government, it is to effectuate the mode by the means of which time will progress to the moment or to the event when the State of Israel will be definitively and irreversibly determined as a dictatorship. On our part, it is a struggle for modulating the future time against the figures of the judicial reform aiming at shooting their arrow to its target in a way that will prove irreversible, an unstoppable telos. The horror of a fascist coup is a unilateral, irreversible arrow. It might be reversible through a bloody counter-coup that will be perceived by the State as illegitimate and illegal, and even then, such a bloody course might not suffice.

If we define this as a singular moment, then we must inquire whether the present moment, as it figured in the parliament, is such a singular moment or whether it too may be removed from its singularity, from its brutal temporal articulation as a definitive "before" and a definitive "after." The concept of singularity here is inspired by its definition in Astrophysics and in the study of Artificial Intelligence: the moment the black hole is surpassed or the moment in which AI will have acquired artificial self-consciousness, a moment in which it is no longer possible to determine reality. In our context, while it is possible to determine this moment, it is no longer possible to change it, and to some extent, to predict its aftermath; for under dark fascist regimes, nobody is safe, not even the leader, who from that singular moment onward lives under permanent paranoia which is intrinsic to the situation. Take, for example, the people in Iran, Russia, or in the past, in Germany, the Soviet Union, and in Arab States who, following such a singular moment, were unsuccessful at bringing down totalitarian regimes, with agendas from the left, the right, or religious fundamentalism.

It follows that the protestation is acting within the opponent's temporal scheme, within its temporal orbit, as was cruelly attested by today's event in the parliament. The question then remains how to overcome this foretold destiny dictated by the opponent to both sides, if we animate it as a factor possessing "consciousness" that directs its agents' actions to serve its interests, and how to tilt the balance toward its historical exhaustion. Another inevitable question is whether time itself is an opponent of the protest. Is the final act of the telos its enemy? We are faced with multiple possibilities of temporal configurations; therefore, we must formulate a strategy in relation to the opponent's mode of organization of its own temporal axis. The opponent is simultaneously constructing the temporal tunnel, directing temporality within time, forcing the protesters to move along the same tunnel toward its final destination, thereby thrusting them into another tunnel, which is both the tunnel of the time-of-protest and the time-of-the-fall of democracy.

The protesters are thus trapped in the opponent's temporality like an insect that a cat is toying with before it finally decides to swallow it. Is this not a maltreatment of temporality? The very maltreatment of all treatment? The protesters are faced with a paradoxical situation: on the one hand, they understand that the ongoing event is a poisonous arrow aimed at a specific future target, albeit the various apparently innocent declarations of the cat guarding the milk and the victimized mouse, such as, "trust us, we shall defend democracy, defend the LGBT's"; but we understand all too well what has occurred in Poland, in Hungary, and in other countries, where fascism defeated democracy through a cynical abuse of democratic logic. On the other hand, we understand the particular significance of the present historical moment: this is our heroic moment, the protesters' moment.

Through these lines, I am attempting to somewhat clarify the temporal moment and to imply an alternative, metaphysical relation to it, one that might perhaps ease the burden and even reinforce the moment. If we are trapped in a temporal tunnel leading to such a final, deadly end, then we are also possibly trapped in an emotional dissonance regarding a predetermined future. I choose to define this emotional state as "the paradox of despair."

For political action, notably when incited by protest, revolution, and regime resistance, occurs on a temporal continuum of despair. Such is the case also in less acute situations, for the political aspires to change an unlikely situation which has no desire to change, or be changed. Despair, as a derivative of the temporal moment, plays a crucial role in political action and needs to be addressed with extra sensitivity, rather than with disregard for its emancipatory potential. Despair, at least as understood on its temporal axis and when it assembles a critical mass of protesters rising up all at once, may serve as raw material, rather than an obstacle. This potentiality of grouping desperate individuals under the same cluster of hope is materializing these days through the various technological applications, from Facebook to WhatsApp groups. But it does not stop there; it is also manifested through boisterous demonstrations as well as the wondrous march from Tel Aviv to Jerusalem. From the consciousness of despair springs the heroic act, namely, an act that performs a retroactive amendment in the present time. With this teleological logic leading to despair, the protest re-inscribes the event in view of the future experience. It is the imagined experience of a future Israel, as if we have leaped five years forward through a time machine. We must look upon the present political situation from its future perspective, and from the future perspective, ask ourselves what we could have done that we did not do. We must already visualize this retrospective view from the dark, despondent future, as if we were already deeply buried in fascism. A definitive acknowledgment of an anticipated failure may remove us from its ultimate tragic outcome and transport us to the heroic time that alters the future moment that is yet to come. Then the future will have been amended. To quote from the beautiful poem by William Blake, "The Mental Traveler": "For the Eye altering alters all."

July 24, 2023.

Note

1 What the government had termed as "judicial reform," its liberal opponents have named "coup de regime."

Chapter 7

The Pre-Theological YOU

Reading Psalm 23 following October 7

Precedent

One month following the manifestation of "where deep calls to deep/ in the roar of Your cataracts"[1] (Psalms, 42: 8) on October 7, 2023, I uploaded on various social networks a series of fragments from Psalms, excluding God's name, the one whose presence – from the poet's perspective – is usually his absence. Through the fragmented quotations I expressed, were the growing horror as well as the growing need for hope, the hope lying beyond the salvation of the beyond.

In a short statement on November 25th, I added a condensation to the 23rd verse from Psalms, brought herewith as a **primary version** of the following text. Among the respondents, some expressed surprise at the effacement of God, the effacement of the "main point," and surprise at what the text understands here as an inward shifting of the You ["ata" in Hebrew] in the verse, to its object position, the Hebrew conjunctive preposition "et."[2]

The discourse on the networks has generated an investigation presented herewith in two additional versions. The **secondary version** has the character of an academic-thesis-lecture, which I delivered on December 23, 2023, at the Bezalel Academy of Art and Design, within the framework of the seminar "Discourse Under War." The **tertiary version**, whose character is topological, was written as a lecture I gave on May 10, 2024, within a seminar on continental philosophy.

It has been over six months since the Israeli hostages were in captivity. The wording in this text is stuttering its time. The present time is not one for reading, nor for writing, nor for thought, and nor for summoning,[3] but it does call for reflection on our own impossibility to be present in it. To reflect from within the catastrophe enveloping us all, as well as reflect upon the envelope itself and its constitution.

The present wording is a self-formulation of the failure to explain the You and the hopeful expectation from it. All that the wording does is to weigh this formulation, which itself is a failure as a formulation, at the same time that it forms and explicates it. This *folding*, in which the formulation both explains

DOI: 10.4324/9781003667339-7

the failure as well as fails to explain it, demonstrates for us the entangled possibility to encounter the You as a personal hope when it is being locked within a predominant signifier – You ["ata"], the predominant word in the language and the foundation of the Hebrew conjunctive preposition "et."

In order to be able to adopt a somewhat exterior view, to escape to some extent the suffocation of the lingual topology and the amalgam of philosophical concepts that are intermittently shrinking and widening in the present text, the wording needs to forget them so that it may remember.

Primary Version

"Though I walk through a valley of the shadow of death, I fear no harm, for You are with me" (Psalms, 23:4). The definitive belief that there is a certain "You" guarding them is what enables the ones walking through the valley of the shadow of death to trust in hope and remedy. We shall continue being the same instrumental "You" for them.

Secondary Version

1   In the morning a momentarily-anonymous woman howled at the TV broadcaster witnessing the moment of her ruin, in a pleading voice, for *someone* to deviate from being *him* to being *You*, someone who will come to the rescue, anyone, man or woman, one or several, whoever, the army, the soldiers, the State, the police, the government, the people, the UN; she howled through her conversation with the broadcaster to all those who might be listening. From her innermost personal place, she cried out to the most public one to become the most personal to come and save her and her family. The moment of her being anonymous she no longer is, for no one comes to the rescue. The time of her death precedes the death of the conversation. She is no longer she. She is you ["at," the Hebrew singular, feminine]. You who is no longer alive. And then another she, and another one, and another, meet their deaths. A death continuum of those who lived their lives under the assumption of a shielding You. The State. The Israel Defense Forces. The government and its governance.

2   She who cried out the death of her innocence at the broadcaster and his audience. Her example is herewith abstract and representative, an image of the truth represented in words, which she expressed through her personal voice. A voice perceived as inclusive by those who did not know her, when she called for immediate assistance from an omnipresent, singular You, not an abstract entity. Here she is an all-embracing figure, representing all the women, men, and children, who cried via WhatsApp "where are You?" A cry at a country deserting its people, its settlers, and the Kibbutz. She cried being aware of the political; she cried from her own place, from

a most specific place. And specificity always has something of the political. Specificity in relation to other political possibilities of specificity. Various sorts of specificity are linked to various modes of relating to the other and the other's political space. This particular woman is voicing her plea from a particular form of being Israeli, the Kibbutz; albeit, this form has lost its significance concerning its social realization, maintaining solely the significance of its ideological cortex. But even if this cortex is rather thin, as an image, within the Israeli space, it still carries a message, a message of promise.

3 She lived in the Gaza Envelope, in the Kibbutz, the symbol of the socialist and/or secular and/or democratic Zionism. She lived within the secular Ashkenazi stereotype, greatly despised by the ongoing regime for several decades now, marked prior to the catastrophic Shabbat as the privileged defeated Israel, as an obsolete, no longer relevant form of Israeli Jewishness, in view of the apparent national necessity to return to the "authentic," pious, and Jewishness to a form of dialectical religiosity beyond all dialectics.
This is the moment to ask for forgiveness regarding the beyond of the metaphysical discussion, but also to acknowledge the fact that we are forever in the midst of the same metaphysical discussion. What is piousness emerging from its dialectics to its beyond? It is religiosity that uses the absence of God in a dialectical manner that is also characterized by or translated into an impossibility to represent that skips over the dialectics in order to reinforce faith (what I have referred to as the theology of the "why-because": why believe? Because; and why because? Because God). Let us tarry within that primary presence of the You in general and the divine You in particular.
    For several years now, the same Israeli particularity is perceived by one side of the political spectrum (and perhaps not any longer) as not loyal enough to the concept national; hence, to the Jewish spirit, or to a fundamental kernel of that Jewishness, as if Jewishness meant faithfulness to itself, faithfulness to the confidence in itself and in its God. Why not the opposite? Perhaps Jewishness means rather being unfaithful to itself? Independence from its God? Irresponsiveness on the part of its God?

4 I would like to explore an ancient, and perhaps even a current, modern form of being Israeli, following another question that has occupied my mind almost associatively, regarding the hope in the hearts of the hostages in captivity, most of whom are members of the Kibbutzim in the Gaza Strip. An association, which has perhaps allowed me a Freudian contact with the Israeli repression of Jewishness. Both a historical as well as a structural repression. Through this envelope, dwelling between the question of repressed hope within the ideological theologies of Jewishness and its characterization, I am revolving in a theological, or rather

a-theological, circle without really completing it, in the a-theological within the heart of the theological. Namely, the circles on which I choose to tread are circles of stutter, meander, and probe, rather than completion. A preliminary inquiry into something which may not allow the possibility of being inquired, the You component. All this under the assumption that all components are atoms of the same molecule – the molecule of the political – whether the atom is theological, a-theological, or civic. Furthermore, the same molecule is floating in an ontological sphere which demands investigation as well, insofar as it may be rimmed within the ontology of the You. The lingual ontology of the You. From this aspect, the discussion will also indirectly touch upon the question of the representation of the traumatic event, but not of the trauma itself or its momentousness, but rather upon the moment of expecting rescue, or the unresponsive Other, in the event.

5 Back to the mode of secular Zionism, marked by the Bibist-Kahanist machine with utmost insolence, the betrayal of Zionism. What really matters is not whether the Jewishness that preceded Zionism was characterized along the lines I am about to describe, but rather that Zionism aspired to provide meaning and a solution to what it perceived then as the main characteristic of Jewishness, as it imagined it. And the image was: the helplessness of the Jew dependent on his faith in a God who does not deliver, whose Rabbis expect Him to defer the political in relation to the world. The sole "political" required was intra-congregational. Within the characterization of this imaging, which is also a Jewish self-stereotyping, there is a key component for its understanding and even for the understanding of monotheism as a whole, with its institutions, beliefs, theologies, and various religious denominations, regarding the dialectics of the relation between the subject and the Other. In question is the concealment of the face of the big Other.

6 From a certain reading of the fundamental text – the Bible – which eventually developed into what has become "Judaism," the absence of God during a national crisis is a pivotal axis. Or rather, the presence of the axis of absence. Many biblical verses describing occurrences of destruction or salvation echo the situation of the Jews and the Israelites in exile, where the Biblical canon was finally edited and sealed. One may read these biblical texts in a double manner, namely, proceed with the reading along two *concurrent* dimensions (not necessarily in a dialectical manner leading to a solution or the subjection of one side or the other). On the one hand, as an expression of trust in God and his power of salvation, but on the other hand, rather as an expression of hopelessness and supplication for the withdrawn God to extract himself from his silence and provide a remedy. Does His absence attest to his non-being?

To a certain extent, the reading of these two synchronic aspects in the biblical text echo the spirit of history along the lines of Walter Benjamin's angel of history. A growing inscription of salvation as an ideological rewriting of perpetual destruction. Therefore, we must push further and see whether these expressions are a theological dimension beyond the political one, or within it? Also, in regard to the biblical source, the theological is not necessarily external to the political order. First, because the divine metaphor is a re-inscription of the metaphor of a ruling king. Two forms of metaphors inscribe each other. The king is God, and God is king. And both are forms of domination presumed to represent a protective, supporting factor. The public institutions during biblical times constituted a form of *augmented* other presumed to support the kingdom's inhabitants, and so their collapse also meant the collapse of the divine metaphor – of the rule in God's image. In the biblical text, this is manifested in a way in which the textual metaphor under the image of God, Yahweh, speaks of its own circular collapse. These are metaphors because they are imaginary forms of the protective essence of an augmented other or otherness in the ontological sense, beyond any form of an *ordinary other*.

God himself informs his people through Abraham and Moses that during certain periods of time, he will conceal his face from them. Though the blame lies mostly with the people, as Hilary Putnam points out in his analysis of Buber's conception of friendship; some of the ancient Hebrew sages ("Hazal") indicated that at times God operates in disjunctive manners regarding human flaws. He is wanting. Or, the perpetration occurs without him interfering or coming to the rescue, he is resting in his corner, an undisturbed onlooker. His unresponsiveness has become a central component of Judaism, also in the Rabbinical-Talmudic version, as an alternative component to God's image, or in the Kabbalah, which places the relation between God and the human being in a deeply entangled dialectics of null, in which the null becomes an affective raw material for the mystical experience.

The envelope of the *nothingness* subverting the *being* within the dynamics of these Kabbalistic dialectics generated, for example, the mystical sedition of Sabbatai Zevi, which Gershom Scholem considered as a proto-Zionist, antinomian revolution. The laws of the Torah and the Halakhah have lost their power of camouflaging the void of God's absence. Then, we witness a metamorphosis of this nothingness into the Jew acting in the political sphere for him/herself, and him/herself alone. The birth of the political realness toward the next step of Zionism.

7   This dimension, the autonomous fantasy of Zionism, has recently cracked as a result of the schemes of the so-called judicial reform tainted by a theologocentric momentum (even if it is manipulated toward the takeover of sovereignty by a bunch of criminals). Toward bringing back the Jew

subjected to the Kabbalistic dialectics of nothingness. The abandonment of the Kibbutzim with no defense line, in favor of the messianic settlements, which enabled the disaster of October 7, was more than symbolic, for it did not occur outside the political context in Israel on the eve of the "judicial reform." An abandonment that is now seeking and expected to make amends. To make amends through being for the abducted hostages that very You that they expect us to be. The You that will bring them back. For a better understanding of You, and its variations in Judaism and in Zionism, let us return to the biblical text.

8   Back to the biblical origin of a demand for response from You or an augmented You. Following is my contribution to the question of hope within the predicament of the hostages in Hamas captivity, the hope that there is *us* looking out for them, even if they are not aware of it (except when, on rare occasions, they are exposed to the media and witness our concern). I am wondering about the historical, theological, and pre-theological traits of the Jews and Israelis in Hamas captivity. How is basic human hope related to hope when slanted into a specific historic-cultural space? Is there a possibility that a "You" exists as a source of hope for the hostages in Gaza?

9   I would like to evoke the pre-theological shift of Zionism, as well as the current downfall of this shift. (A shift that originated in the disenchantment with the divine "You" as a source of salvation in the diaspora, and culminated with the Holocaust.) I propose a reading of a specific Psalm, inspired by Levinas, Buber, Benveniste, and Lacan, regarding the moment of the "You" in the lives of the human being in general, and of the Jew and the Israeli, in particular. By this, I mean the acknowledgment of a pre-theological, and even pre-existential dimension, in our political and even religious and spiritual lives, and to propose that the theological, the political, the social, and the existential are an exterior envelope of a *primary verbal nucleus*. Of a single word. Also, to propose that there is a non-dialectic cut between the envelope and the source. Thus goes the central verse of the 23rd Psalm: "Though I walk through a valley of the shadow of death, I fear no harm, for You are with me."

10   The definitive belief that there is a certain "You" guarding them is what enables the ones walking through the valley of the shadow of death to trust in hope and remedy. The possibility to say You, to address it. Following the deception of You during the catastrophic occurrence of October 7, our task now is to be the "You" for them. Contrary to the assertion that the main point in the 23rd Psalm is the presence of God, I propose – perhaps drawing from Buber and Benvetiste[4] – that this God is founded on a *"You" which ontologically precedes him*. This is the main point beyond the main point. Perhaps the beyond sought after by the theologians. Transcendent *to God Himself.*

The You is first and foremost lingual, before it is theological, psychological, existential, social, or political. Or, one is trapped in the abyss of the word as a *signifier devoid of the world*. For the plea through the word "You" lies within the word itself. And then the rest follows. Therefore, the theological cannot precede the word You. Namely, there is something that carries the word You prior to clarifying who that You might be. The plea must reflect upon itself and recognize the existence of the You. It might be – drawing from Lacan and Levinas – that the You implies an ontological dimension even preceding the lingual and non-theological. The theological seeks to reduce this dimension to the image of God. Namely, to an imaginary, mythological, immaterial, and abstract dimension.

11   My discussion is an elaboration of the work on the concept of trauma, drawing from Lacan's thought, as was discussed in one of the chapters of my book, *Critical Theology*,[5] the idea that in the heart of the traumatic event lies the absence of the You or the Other that was expected to provide support during its occurrence. A more difficult effect to bear is the physical or mental injury caused by the perpetrator. This is my reference point, leading to the question of hope. Namely, to proceed toward the question of hope lying beyond the traumatic event, the pronounced expression of hope in Psalms 23 will assist me.

1A psalm of David.
  Yahweh is my shepherd;
  I lack nothing.
2He makes me lie down in green pastures;
  He leads me to still waters in places of repose;
3He renews my life;
  He guides me in right paths
  as befits His name.
4Though I walk through the valley of the shadow of death
  I fear no harm, for You are with me;
  Your rod and Your staff – they comfort me;
5You spread a table before me in full view of my enemies;
  You anoint my head with oil;
  my drink is abundant.
6Only goodness and steadfast love shall pursue me
  all the days of my life,
  and I shall dwell in the house of Yahweh
  for many long years.

"I fear no harm, for You are with me" states the poet and gives David's name as a lyrical reference. What does the figuration of the word You in the heart of this psalm signify? A minute analysis of a single word from the entire Bible is indeed a pretentious attempt to decipher a few thousand years of Judaism, including its Zionist moment and the breaking point of October 7. Evidently, to over-specify the explanation would be perceived as overshooting. But since this specific word does not contain an explanation, analyzing it is rather an attempt to provide us with a "quilting point" in relation to its imaginary modes of presentation in the Jewish tradition as well as in the Israeli one. A kind of card in an imaginary game of cards. A foothold. Thus, this does not constitute any suggestion of significance but rather the opposite, a non-disclosure singling out an insignificant, inexplicable moment, concealed in its persistence not to be exposed, for the secret of its essence is the secret itself. We offer ourselves neither an explanation nor any logic, but a mere acknowledgment of the meaninglessness in the heart of the Jewish and the Israeli experience. A conceptual analysis of conceptual and verbal components posited against each other, for we are found in a spongy reality, a mass that has swallowed up conceptual entities, such as the existence of God or His death, or the You, or Jewishness, or Zionism, a conceptually indistinctive mass.

12   Back to the Psalm.
To begin with, this psalm preaches the trivial, but not the obvious: *that it is made of words*, *that it is a writing*. And as such, it is a demonstration of the relation of the words to themselves as words and as a field of interliterality, rather than one of experience. And if we do consider it as an experience, then it is the experience of the word's encounter with itself. Within this theater of the word, we imagine a human experience.

The psalm declares that it is a *psalm of David*. Truly bad translators. But what is a translation in the best if not the worst case, if not its desire to attain the secret of the written word conversing with itself in the original language? These words may be read, "a psalm of/by David," but what they really show is that they are directed to another, already existing, written space, the one attributed or dedicated to King David. Scholars estimate that these texts date from the end of the First Temple and the Babylonian Exile, or the beginning of the Second Temple, namely, that they refer to a "Davidian" textual space known to the reader. In effect, not to the reader, but to the very words of that Davidian textual space, and for this reason, this is a psalm of David. The written experience is not necessarily a naïve documentation of a human experience; it is charged with words and corresponds to the mode through which *language itself* experienced the human experience as *verbal*.

13   The poet poses two forms of the human relation to God. The first is the metaphor of a flock led by its shepherd, the second, to some extent also metaphorical, refers to the relation between the king and his God, or between a guest and his host. Between the two, there is a blurred dissolve, as well as a slippage of confidence in the shepherd or the host, against a

howling voice on the brink of despair. Some scholars read the psalm as an expression of positive faith in God. However, biblical scholar Shamai Galander, in his comprehensive study, *The Religious Experience in the Book of Psalms*, targets a more existential direction, in opposition to this one. Such is his reading of the Book of Ecclesiastes as well, of a proto-atheistic text about a reality devoid of any transcendence, appeasing, or redeeming dimension. Similarly, the prominent scholar Edward Greenstein's reading in his *Job: A New Translation*.[6] These are books expressing distress and despair regarding the very possibility of God being a source of redemption, and even a clandestine recognition that reality has no divine horizon. A proto-atheism concealed in the biblical atheism, which is perhaps the derivative of the transcendent distancing of God from reality due to his omnipresent infiniteness even beforehand, and in concurrence with the Aristotelian metaphysics. Or, the transcendent distancing may be an expression of the theological envelope being the one that "senses" the existence of a *cut* between it and the word in its pre-theological existence. The pleas to God, abounding with praise and glorification for Yahweh expected to be almighty (a maximalism which ultimately crucifies God), do not necessarily indicate a belief in redemption, but rather a culmination of distress, when the author about to meet his death cries out, begging for a miraculous salvation. Hence, one must be careful not to read the desperate cry present in the synchronicity of this dual dialectics as confidence that God will come to the rescue, or that he even exists.

14 In the middle of the psalm, there is a rhetorical shift from relating to God in the third person to a direct address in the second person. This verse is also unique in that it postulates a situation of optionality. Thou I... But this optionality is not only an impossible possibility, but also a depiction of a situation in which the possibility exists. This rhetorical shift is partially juxtaposed to the shift from the shepherd metaphor to the monarchial one. Though I... for You are with me. The appeal through the pronoun "You" indicates both an intimate affinity and a real cry for help.

   Following Buber, I regard the I–You relations present herewith as a pre-theological situational structure. Namely, the appeal to God in this verse is a moment in which the interior discourse of the text changes and grants us an aperture to some secret truth in it, beyond its theological-ideological rhetoric.

15 How does ideology figure here? In Althusser's thought, the subject responding to the State apparatus imagines himself to be responding to himself, a position he terms "interpellation." Here, the interpellation does not refer to the believer but to God. It is rather a counter-interpellation in which the subject appeals to a big You, a personal address of the subject to his big Other. In this way, the subject positions himself in an I–You

relation that is basically lingual, but this lingual condition enables him/her to constitute his/her subjectivity. At the same time, this constitution is implicated in a counter-counter-interpellation which is fundamentally the *dissolution* of this subjectivity under an ideological order, in which the Other disengages from its own constitution as such and is presented henceforth as the agency generating an address in the subject.

This ideological-theological envelope is the frame of reference for the events that preceded October 7. The "judicial reform" in Israel seeks to restore the seniority of the political YOU to its theological envelope. If the Zionist project sought to endow the You with political meaning, namely to seek a solution, the judicial reform's intent is to reinstate in it an a-political, theological dissolution. The attempt to reconstitute a theocratic regime is part and parcel of establishing a despotic regime in which there is but one shepherd leading his people as he sees fit. Then again, the psalm too offers us a reliance on a singular shepherd. "Your rod and your staff." The psalm is like a *chemical smelt, an amalgam* of the ideological theology with its proto-theological dimension and the envelope of that proto.

Tertiary Version

1   In the morning, a momentarily-anonymous woman howled at the TV broadcaster, witnessing the moment of her ruin, in a pleading voice, for someone to deviate from being **Him** to being **You**, someone who will come to the rescue, anyone, man or woman, one or several, whoever, the army, the soldiers, the State, the police, the government, the people, or the UN; she howled through her conversation with the broadcaster to all those who might be listening. From her innermost personal place, she cried out to the most public one to become the most personal to come and save *her and her family*. Up to that moment, she had been living under her civilian illusion of mutual responsibility, that she is not only *she* but also You, a part of the You men and women, that the Israeli community is a community of a plural You ["atem"] in which the conjunctive "et" activates all of its members concurrently, even though what motivates the relations between them, the social relation itself, might remain obscure. In question is not only an adhesive factor but also a machine that sets a course of events in motion, an engine. Perhaps, this is why the woman turned to the television machine to set in motion a course of action, reignite the engine, under its illusory energy. But this addition might also imply a sedition, emerging from this illusion in which the plural *YOU* is presumed to be saved by another plural *YOU*. They also presumed a utopian relation with their Palestinian neighbors that they share a common path toward a form of plural You, albeit extrinsic (following a lecture held by a scholar of Classical Studies, Prof. Vered Lev Kenaan, on the Greek "Xenia" as the

"ahsaniya" [אכסנייה][7] – the Hebrew word having a relation of Xenia with the Greek one – of the "xenos" [both foreigner and host], weaved together in the word hospitality.)

2 *Where are you* ["at," feminine singular]? (I address her, that same she. I will address You, ["at"]. Am I addressing the word you? Am I addressing who you are beyond the word "you"? Does the word you ["at"] annihilate the way of the conjunctive "et" to you?

3 *You* dwelled in the Gaza Envelope, in the Kibbutz, the symbol of the socialist and/or secular and/or democratic Zionism, within the secular Ashkenazi stereotype greatly despised by the ongoing regime for several decades now. *You*, the subject of this stereotyping, or rather the object of this image, whose understanding of your fellow-people's space as strictly human and in accordance with Humanism tradition, is no longer legitimate. Perhaps, humanism, rather than placing the human in the center, places humanity as the position of fellow-people, in opposition to its being a trans-humanist factor. *In opposition* does not necessarily mean a simple contrast but rather a detached, cut-off reflected image. What is the nature of this opposition? Is it possible to offer a disjunction that will cut through its dialectical metaphysics?

The humanistic approach is largely nourished by monotheism. For example, we may find in various modern Jewish thinkers – from Buber and Rosenzweig to Levinas and Heschel – a presentation of the humanistic fellow-other perspective as based on the divine one, and vice versa. From which follows this dual movement is itself the perspective of the fellow-other. Through a more complex topology, it may be contended that the fellow-other is not constituted in relation to God nor to the human, but is itself the relation God – the human being. To some extent, we are both trapped within this complex typology as well as attempting to find a way out of it. On the one hand, we are doubling this typology. On the other hand, we could persist in saying that this topological cord had already been severed, at least by the secular, humanistic side, while the theological-religious side perseveres in it. Is there any feasible situation in which the humanistic project no longer requires leaning on the *beyond* of the fellow-other in order to deepen it? An entity beyond any form of affinity? Is it possible that the humanistic project positions the fellow-otherness on the other itself, namely that the entire weight of the fellow-otherness of the human other derives from its being human, a human being? A person with whom the encounter bears the weight of being related to his/her being a mortal devoid of any mystical or spiritual prosthesis to alleviate the burden that is already too heavy to bear? The burden of objectification is an inherent trait, which is manifested toward the fellow-otherness and inscribed as such.

4   There are attempts in Jewish thought – from Buber[8] onward, under Hegel's
    influence – to introduce a *dialectical space* between humanistic secularism
    in its relation to fellow-otherness and the theological model of the relation
    between the believer and his/her God (Levinas, for example, was caught in
    an interior formulation of a question, while Rabbi Kook took a sound bite
    from the Hegelian sandwich, with his synthetic salami). What does this
    dialectical space mean? It is a space, a gap, impossible to bridge. But since
    the conception remains dialectical, the relation would be,

between
an unbridgeable gap
and
a dialectical relation
or, according to the following scheme:
a higher level of dialectics
between
theological-dialectics and the lack of secular dialectics

or, a parody on the Hegelian *Aufhenbung*:

synthesis + antithesis › synthesis

It follows that the dialectical space ultimately reinforces the theological
position, whose basic postulate is that the humanistic *cannot be but* subjected to the theological. Is there a possibility to escape this dialectical
trap, when it represents a fundamental dialectical model in the Old
Testament, as well as in the New Testament and the Koran thereafter? It is
a receptacle-like dialectic in the sense that it contains both the dialectic
(theological) relation itself as well as the non-dialectic (strictly humanistic
or secular) one, thereby creating a super-dialectic (monotheism). "Love
your fellow as yourself" [Leviticus, 19: 18) is a continuation of "the whole
Israelite community" [19: 2], which are not situated as single humanistic
expressions but within a dialectical model, accompanied by the recurring
divine ending, "I Yahweh am your God." In between, there exists a
super-dialectic relation of a superior authority both producing the "the"
interactions and inserting itself as Divinity within them, since they are
dialectical relations between the human being and his/her fellow people.
"You shall not take vengeance or bear a grudge against your countrymen.
Love your fellow as yourself: I am Yahweh" (Leviticus, 19:18). The objectification is neither of the person facing me nor even of Yahweh facing me,
but of the very dialectics between the dialectical and the non-dialectical.
Then, a wonder of wonders, the dialectical machine, perhaps because it is
teleological leading to the end of history, also leads to the annulment of
the dialectics itself and the victory of the theological (the passage from an
inclusive dialectical theology that had been instrumental to theology to

pure theology). When dialectics is an engine, it is always a dialectical form leading to its annulment, at least within the fantasy of the dialectical machine itself.

5   *You* ["at"] are the one who prior to the catastrophic Shabbat signified the privileged, defeated Israel, the obsolete, no longer relevant form of Israeli Jewishness, in view of the apparent national necessity to return to the "authentic" and pious Jewishness, to a form of dialectical religiosity beyond all dialectics, as reflected in the tautology of an Israeli popular song: "If you believe/you're not afraid to lose your faith." The believer who believes that he/she believes, in this dialectics in which faith is stabilized through fear, with its unopposed opposite, which is faith. Yes, the end result is faith.

Thesis + thesis >> thesis

So what is faith that emerges from within the dialectics beyond it? I maintain that it is religiosity that utilizes God's absence/responsiveness in a prevaricate manner, that is also characterized by or translated into an impossibility of representation; skipping the dialectics to reinforce faith (what I have termed, the theology of the "why-because": why believe? Because).

6   You tarried in a split second that lasted an eternity, a brutal eternity, in an infinite irresponsiveness of an absent You, an absence that augmented the neediness for the "the" relations. The neediness for that Zionist You present in the absence of the omni-impotent, omni-absent Jewish God. *You* are the one who cried out the death of your credulity through the broadcaster and his audience; but through the example read herewith, you become an abstract, representative example, a veritable image, represented herewith in words uttered through your most personal voice. A voice perceived by all the listeners who did not know you, as a common, urgent appeal for help, addressed to an urgent, singular You, and not to an abstract entity. Here, you are an all-embracing being, for too many men, women, and children who cried through the social apps, the radio, and the television, "Where are You?". A cry at the country that had abandoned you and your fellow members of your Kibbutz.

There is something of the political in your cry, for you are a cry emerging from your place, from a very specific place. In specificity, there is always something of the political. Specificity in relation to other possible political specificities. Various specificities under various modes of interrelations regarding the fellow-people, as well as the political space and the space of the fellow-other.

7   Namely, we are concerned with various relational relations with the relativity of the relation. As if there were never a single, *linear* relational

relation, a single level of the I-You relation. As if we were forever caught in a tri-dimensional topology of relational relations or of various political possibilities of ideological relational relations of the I-You. Accordingly, the pole of the relation I-You is not in opposition to the Buberian I-It relation, because the I-You is not a mere natural human structure but an instrument in a comprehensive structure housing an ideological logic.

Lacan criticized Buber's dual existentialism of the I-You, suggesting that between the two there is the big Other.[9] It seems that the more we delve into the I-You relations as antagonistic to the I-It, we seem to sink more deeply into the tri-dimensional typology of *sampling* a specific Buberian I-You from many I-You *possible specificities*. Within the very I-You relation, there exists a relational option for another, specific relational form of I-You. When I refer to You in a primary natural manner, I am actually choosing one cultural-structural option from the I-You relations; hence, I am always in a relational relation, rather than in a direct one to the You comprising the "the" as such. As we shall see, we are in fact dealing with *four* dimensions, for the three are joined by the *synchronic* one that sets in motion all the tri-dimensional specificities, as it may happen or may be read in what is written, when the syntax of a sentence is such that every single word in it is a synchronic activation of this tri-dimensionality of the various forms of the relational relations leading to four dimensions. Furthermore, I would like to clarify that the multidimensionality of these specificities does not mean that they are philosophically, theologically, existentially, and even syntactically-linguistically speaking, equal. Namely, any possible formulation of a sentence is synchronically dependent on the subject, but the *specificity of what is still possible* remains firm and abiding. Such is the case of the verse quoted from Psalms, in which the word *YOU* may function as God, as a mere lingual you, as a You comprising the conjunction, as the pronoun You, as an empty signifier, and so forth. All of these forms exist synchronically, but in between them all, there is a cut. No dialectical relations, but topological ones. Not similar to a simple Möbius strip or Klein bottle, but to a strip cut by a Guillotine blade at several points. *An interrupted dialectic.*

8 I have endowed you [the woman] herewith with the "the" pertinent to you, I have placed you in a lingual I-you [singular, feminine] relation, along an all-encompassing lingual axis, in your most personal, most concrete address, which is the general formulation of this most personal privacy, and so the most personal is but one formulation within the multidimensionality of the sense of definiteness of the "et" in language, in various conjunctions of the same being of the "et" but at the infinitesimal point not leading to nothing but to the word leading to itself,

the word > inquiring > itself

in the affinity between the very word and itself within the multidimensionality of the word in which the word is ingrained. Then, the article "the" in its most personal sense, in its approximation to itself to the very abyss, and to the point of taking its own life within itself, recognizes itself as a formation of the objectification of the word "you" as singular masculine or as singular feminine or as plural masculine or feminine,[10] as multidimensional conjunctions for various possibilities of interpretation, but in a way through which the most personal of the word becomes the most inclusive, universal way to experience the word when the speaker speaks. I say: "I see *the you* [singular, feminine], I see you." By seeing you, I see the word "et" within the conjunction of the sentence as positioning the objectification of the word "you" in its encounter with its inclusiveness. Hence, you are experienced through the sentence that is the most sensitive to you as personal and to your inclusive *terminal* within the language.

9 This specific woman, *who has been designated herewith as the inclusive you*, voiced her plea from a particular form of being Israeli, the Kibbutz; albeit, this form has lost its significance concerning its social realization, maintaining solely the significance of its ideological cortex. Even if this cortex is rather thin, as an image, within the Israeli space, it still carries a message - a message of promise. The cortex of the image is the tree in its emergence in the world, not only as an image but also as a border with a non-tree world, and even if the tree discards, its bark will still hold on to a re-emerging of it in the world. Such is the word You in the singular, feminine or masculine, as the cortex of the inclusive essence of the specific You that I encounter; and even if the Kibbutz cortex is what has apparently remained under the socialist display, the cortex in both cases, is still the clinging of the image of the thing to its encounter with the world. Whether the word You [singular, masculine] is the inclusive display of its personality or the word Kibbutz is the apparent display as cortex, both are still the borders of this dividing wall between the image and the world. Not the image as casualness masking something but as *the image which is the essence of the thing* without any *Real* behind it. An eternal order of the *Imaginary* with no *Symbolic* and no *Real*. An Imaginary clinging to bordering cortexes with the non-image. Hence, both the personal and the inclusive word "You," as well as the word "Kibbutz," are doing their utmost to be the clinging cortexes in relation to the world which is not them. And these cortexes encounter other ones. And in its synchronic multidimensionality, it is possible to understand each cortex under various interpretive discourses. It remains to be asked whether the word *YOU* [masculine] will sustain itself as such when aspiring to become itself or whether it will attach itself to another word. The word God.

10 The question concerns the historical, the theological, and the proto-theological traits of the feeling of hope when addressing the fellow-other through the word. What is between the fundamental human hope and the

hope that extends within a specific historical-cultural space? Is hope solely a personal, existential thing? Or does it depend on a tri-dimensional structure, which includes the relations of the encounters with fellow-others, under the two-dimensional space that doubles itself within the historical and cultural stratification?

The question relates to the possibility that there exists a "You" [masculine], as a source of hope. That You-person, which is potentially You, and then inscribes that it is inscribed as a word-You [masculine], which is the entirety of the You [masculine] itself emerging from his operating on my behalf, giving hope.

Such is the case in Psalms 23.

"You are with me." In the simplicity of the word "you." The presence of the word You which is with me, is at the base of the psalm. You are with I. The word You enunciates the subjectivization toward the one who is You. You are what you are. The enunciation of the word You is what creates the word You, and in being enunciated, it operates with me. It is with I, the one who is both enunciating and enunciated.

11   I, You [singular masculine], and He. I, You [singular feminine], and He. I, you [singular feminine], and She. The voice of a prompt howl, prompting each feminine and masculine one of us to be a feminine and a masculine You. A howl emerging from the most personal to the most inclusive place that will rise to its most personal to its most You, from a *covert* syntactical pronoun to an overt syntactical *present*.

The ending is rather a quandary:

Does the covert second-person pronoun conceal within it the concept of the absolute other, as the product of the word *HE*, and is then charged under the You?

Does the word "I" address the word "You", in a sentence such as "I see that you are helping me, the I"? In what way the exterior word "I" of the speaking person addresses the interior word in a sentence as its object, in the constitutional relations of "I" <> I?

Does the word I address the You [singular masculine], and positions it on the bi-directional axe You-pronoun, which both constitutes and is constituted vis-à-vis the You-word? "You" <> You.

And then there is the encounter between the axe <> and the axe <>.

And there, between the two axes, does "I" address himself and the "You" himself, and do both self-addresses address each other, within the address of the "I" to the web of these interactive addresses?

Is there an answer to any of these questions?

Does a response to the YOU address of the hostages in captivity that we shall save them exist?

The quandary and the questions constitute the beginning of a response.

Notes

1 All the biblical quotations are taken from the New JPS Translation, 2nd edition, Philadelphia, 1999. The term "The Lord" appearing in the various verses has been altered to "Yahweh".

2 [In Hebrew, "אַתָּה" is the singular-masculine "You" and is pronounced "ata". "אַתְּ" is the singular-feminine "You" and is pronounced "at". "אֶת" ("et") is the Hebrew conjunctive preposition that connects the verb with the definite object, marked in Hebrew by the letter "he" ("הֵא") which is pronounced "ha", e.g.: "Ani ohel **et ha-**tapuah", (I'm eating the apple). The author establishes an ontological relation between the three].

3 ["To summon" in Hebrew is "Lezamen" ("לְזַמֵּן"), same root as the word "time" - "zman" ("זְמַן")].

4 Émile Benveniste, *Problems in General Linguistics*, vol. 1, trans. Mary Elizabeth Meek. Coral Gables, Florida: University of Miami, 1971.

5 Itzhak Benyamini, *Critical Theology*, Tel Aviv: Resling Publishing, 2022 [in Hebrew].

6 Edward L. Greenstein, *Job: A New Translation*, Yale University Press, 2019.

7 Literally: hostelry, hospice.

8 Martin Buber, *I and Thou*, New York: Scribner's Sons, 1970.

9 Jacques Lacan, *The Seminar, Book III: The Psychoses*, NY: WW Norton, 1997.

10 In Hebrew "ata," "at," "atem," and "aten," respectively.

Chapter 8

Netanyahu's Anxiety Machine
Afterword – October 16, 2023

The Hamas attack on Israel on October 7, 2023, was the most catastrophic event in Jewish and Israeli existence since the Holocaust. An event full of horror, brutality, and terror, both for the direct victims as well as for the population of Israel at large. In what follows, I intend to do a retrospective reading of Israeli anxiety, up until its current peak. The perception is not a causal one by which one event led to another. Rather, it demonstrates the understanding of anxiety as the raw material that Israeliness is made of. A raw material that, after October 7, has had a staggering effect on Jews, both in Israel and abroad. I wish to emphasize the manner in which anxiety is not only a psychological phenomenon but also a political one present in the relationship between the government and its citizens, as manifested in my neologism, "the psycho-political" and in the way it is manipulated by a central political figure. I will briefly outline the relationship between the psychological and the political conditions in Israel under Netanyahu's regime during the last decades, hopefully offering the non-Israeli readers a deeper understanding of the Israeli condition.

The primary nature of my theoretical proposal cannot pass over the nonlinear conundrum of these two elements (psychological and political). It is not clear what the cause is and what the effect is, nor what is internal and what is external. In any event, it seems that the element "Netanyahu" has been serving as the supra-navigator of this anxiety in the last decades, in a way that subjugates all forms of Israeliness. A "desire machine" that produces the object, the subject, and the effects in between.

Within the relation between Israeli psychology and its politics, anxiety is both the source of political acts and feelings of anger and bitterness, as well as the constant object of reference. Anxiety is the pincers that attach the psyche to Israeli politics, and the figure who has been toiling toward the tightening of this relationship purely for his specific personal interests is no other than the Prime Minister of Israel and the leader of the right-wing – Benyamin Netanyahu. He was and still is the superintendent, who dilapidates the building and horrifies its residents so that they may continue to depend on him.

In the last decade, many Israelis, especially in the liberal camp defending the values of democracy and aspiring for peace with the Palestinians and the Arab

DOI: 10.4324/9781003667339-8

world, have been living with an increasingly acute sense that Netanyahu is crushing their values, seeking to transform his regime into autocracy, to eliminate public institutions surveilling the government and the rights of citizens and individuals, and to transform the country into theocracy, while promoting Jewish supremacy over its minorities. Theocracy may not be what he himself desires; nevertheless, he has been aligning with nationalist and racist forces, only to hold on to his government and impede his prosecution following several serious investigations for corruption, including betrayal of principles of national security.

In order to tighten the support around him and incite the persecution of his opponents, from the very start, Netanyahu has effectively shaped the Israeli mentality around the politics of a state of emergency. Netanyahu is a pseudo-psychologist à la Carl Schmitt who creates a constant state of emergency and somehow embodies the Israeli sense of the political. For two decades, Israeli politics has been spinning around one question alone: Bibi or not Bibi. Through his personality, Netanyahu offers a remedy for the disease that he himself brought upon the Israeli psyche. He is both a criminal and a policeman concomitantly.

Thus, Netanyahu's leadership has increasingly exacerbated the feeling of anxiety among Israeli citizens, who were already oscillating between a sense of comfort in their homeland and a sense of loss and disorientation. These, in addition to feelings of uncanniness and alienation rooted in the Jewish exilic soul, which have not faded, albeit the Zionist project professedly offering the Jewish people a stable, secure home. Such is the Israeli "Real."

Netanyahu has turned the Israeli experience ("Israeliness") into "Israelism" (ideology). Within this platform, anxiety is integrated as a dual psycho-politics in which right-wingers are portrayed as content with their lot, homeland lovers, and ideologists, while the leftists are portrayed as whiners and betrayers. This is the divide whose mode of existence in the face of anxiety is shaped by Netanyahu. Both groups are anxious, but each group is marked as having a different position vis-à-vis the Israeli chronic symptom. Netanyahu attacks his political opponents as "sour pickles," demands that they give up their "bourgeois" anxieties, and be happy with their leader and join his nationalist anxiety, so that this anxious joy will lead to unbridled support of his personality and leadership: he demands that they convert their anxieties into love for the so-called omnipotent leader, who instills constant pressure and fear in his loyalists.

The justification for this "joyful" support of Netanyahu is the profound anxiety he imposes on the citizens of Israel by exacerbating the apocalyptic tone regarding imminent war waged by Iran and the Arabs against Israel and the constant state of emergency in which they are supposed to live. Netanyahu positions himself as the one who, on the one hand, points out the cause of anxiety and, on the other, offers a state of constant happiness supposedly stemming from sympathy for his leadership. This is the sole legitimate politics from his point of view and that of his supporters.

Not that this anxiety is unfounded. Israelis do live in constant fear for their present and future existence. Notwithstanding, my concern here is the way in which Netanyahu abuses this anxiety for his personal-political gains, that is, the way in which he steers the energy of this anxiety to mold the Israeli political. As I am convinced that he does not act in compliance with the actual needs of Israel, I believe it is safe to say that he puts Israel in great peril. For example, he has practiced a deliberate policy aimed at weakening the Palestinian Authority and moderate Palestinian forces and strengthening extremist forces such as Hamas, so that he will not lose his right-wing and religious-fundamentalist supporters, who would never agree to the political price he might have to pay in the event of a peace agreement with the more moderate forces.

On October 7, all of this blew up in our faces, literally and radically. I write these lines trembling with infinite anxiety, along with the rest of the Israelis, after the worst and most horrific, unthinkable scenario occurred in the towns, villages, and Kibbutzim surrounding Gaza. As we know, members of the extremist Muslim organization Hamas infiltrated Israeli territory and committed atrocities that even the concept of "war crimes" does not begin to describe. But this operation was also the result of the covert collaboration between Israeli and Palestinian extremists, aimed at preventing a fair solution for the Palestinian problem and peace between the nations. The Palestinian national struggle will be severely harmed by the ongoing war in Gaza, while fascism in Israel has received a shining gift in the form of an all-out war against the Arabs under a pan-Israeli consensus. All the worst anxieties are being materialized far and beyond any imagination that anxiety could have aroused in the average Israeli.

During the current state of emergency, as I write these lines, Netanyahu continues to perform a double-stereophonic operation for the purpose of fortifying his government. On the one hand, he encourages his supporters to attack any tweet that does not endorse his position regarding the war and his responsibility for it, and on the other, he encourages his supporters to demonstrate what I have termed "patriotic anxiety." On the one hand, he encourages a sense of cohesion and brotherhood that means supporting him exclusively, and on the other, he encourages the feelings of anxiety among all Israelis so that he may mark himself as the sole Messiah who has the ability to redeem his people from the object of anxiety.

A part of systematizing anxiety and channeling it in the nationalist direction, the object marked as enemy is not only external but also internal and embodied in a stereotype that Netanyahu and his supporters have been cultivating for a long time – the liberal secular Tel Aviv Ashkenazi: the enemy of the people. Even members of the families of the ones who were brutally abducted by the Hamas and are held prisoners in Gaza, who hold silent street protests for their loved ones, are occasionally accused of being leftists and traitors and are subjected to comments such as "they did a good thing killing all of you in the kibbutzim." But those voicing these opinions, "the bibists," are the object of Netanyahu's anxiety too, the object of his sophisticated design. In effect, we are all shaped through Netanyahu's psychopolitics. The positions of both groups toward him emerge as the solution to the contemporary Israeli psychopolitics, but Netanyahu's supporters are blindly unwilling to acknowledge the fact that he has been degrading the country and the people up (or rather down) to the catastrophe that occurred under his watch.

We live in a period that can be named after Netanyahu, not only because he has led Israel during these years but also because the Israeli mentality and Israeli politics have been reduced to the oscillation between two polar but complementary positions: "Only Bibi" and "Anyone but Bibi"; two formulas and in each one of them is felt the anxiety that the other one arouses. The identities of communities that could not be more remote from Netanyahu's own background – the religious communities and Jews from Islamic countries (Sepharadim) – bearing different forms of anxiety, constitute a solid ground for his manipulations in favor of his personal and political gains. The psychopolitics of each community is regulated by its mode of existential anxiety. A nationalist right-wing politics of Identity that ultimately serves those in power alone.

Bibliography

Althusser, Louis, "Ideology and Ideological State Apparatuses (Notes towards an Investigation)", in *Lenin and Philosophy and Other Essays*, transl. B. Brewster, London: New Left Books, 1971, pp. 127–186.

Aristotle, *Aristotle's Politica*, ed. W. D. Ross, Oxford: Clarendon Press, 1957.

Aristotle, *Metaphysics*, transl. H. Tredennick, Cambridge, MA: Harvard University Press, 1961.

Aristotle, *Politics*, transl. C. D. C. Reeve, Indianapolis: Hackett, 1998.

Balibar, Etienne, "Citoyen sujet", *Cahiers Confrontation*, vol. 20 (Hiver 1989): 23–48.

Balibar, Étienne, *Citizen Subject: Foundations for Philosophical Anthropology*, transl. S. Miller, New York: Fordham University Press, 2016.

Benjamin, Walter, "The Task of the Translator", in *Selected Writings – Vol. 1*, ed. M. Bullock and M.W. Jennings, Cambridge, Mass & London: The Belknap Press of Harvard University Press, 1992, pp. 258–259.

Benjamin, Walter, "Critique of Violence", in *Selected Writings Vol. 1 1913–1926*, ed. M. Bullock and M. Jennings, Cambridge, MA: Harvard University Press, 1996, pp. 236–252.

Benveniste, Émile, *Problems in General Linguistics*, vol. 1, transl. M. E. Meek and C. Gables, Florida: University of Miami, 1971.

Benyamini, Itzhak, *Critical Theology*, Tel Aviv: Resling Publishing, 2022 [in Hebrew].

Buber, Martin, *I and Thou*, New York: Scribner's Sons, 1970.

Derrida, Jacques, *The Gift of Death*, transl. D. Wills, Chicago: University of Chicago Press, 1966.

Derrida, Jacques, "Force of the Law: The Mystical Foundation of Authority", in *Deconstruction and the Possibility of Justice*, ed. D. Cornell, M. Rosenfeld, and D. Gray Carlson, New York and London: Routledge, 1992, pp. 3–67.

Durkheim, Émile, *The Elementary Force of the Religious Life*, transl. J. W. Swain, Mineola, NY: Dover Publications, 2008.

Foucault, Michel, "Qu'est-ce qu'un auteur", *Bulletin de la Société française de philosophie*, 63 anné, no 3, juillet-septembre 1969, pp. 73–104.

Foucault, Michel, *Power/Knowledge: Selected Interviews and Other Writings 1972–1977*, transl. C. Gordon et al., ed. C. Gordon, Brighton: Harvester, 1980.

Freud, Sigmund, "Morning and Melancholy" (1917), SE 14.

Freud, Sigmund, "The Uncanny" (1919), SE 17.

Freud, Sigmund, "Inhibition, Symptom and Anxiety" (1926), SE 20, pp. 217–256.

Freud, Sigmund, "Fetishism", *International Journal of Psychoanalysis 9*, transl. J. Riviere (1928), 161–166.

Freud, Sigmund, "Project for a Scientific Psychology", in *The Origins of Psycho-Analysis: Letters to Wilhelm Fliess, Drafts and Notes: 1887–1902*, ed. J. Masson, transl. J. Strachey et al., New York: Basic Books, 1954, pp. 347–445.

Freud, Sigmund, "Negation" (1925), in *The Standard Edition of the Complete Psychological Works of Sigmund Freud, vol. 19: The Ego and the Id and Other Works*, transl. J. Strachey, London: Hogarth Press, 1961, pp. 235–239.

Freud, Sigmund, *The Interpretation of Dreams*, transl. J. Crick, Oxford: Oxford University Press, 1999.

Gadamer, Hans-Georg, *Truth and Method*, 2nd rev. edition, transl. J. Weinsheimer and D. G. Marshall, New York: Crossroad, 2004.

Greenstein, Edward L., "The Torah as She is Read", *Response* 47 (Winter 1985): 17–40.

Greenstein, Edward L., *Job: A New Translation*, Yale University Press, 2019.

Heidegger, Martin, *On the Way to Language*, San Francisco: Harper San Francisco, 1982.

Heidegger, Martin, *Pathmarks*, ed. W. McNeill, Cambridge: Cambridge University Press, 1998.

Heidegger, Martin, "Der Ursprung des Kunstwerkes", in *Holzwege*, Frankfurt: Klostermann, 2003.

Heidegger, Martin, "The Thing", in *Bremen and Freiburg Lectures*, ed. F.-W. V. Herrmann, transl. A. J. Mitchell, Bloomington, Indiana: Indiana University Press, 2012.

Hendel, Arie (ed.), *Kriat Hameha'a: Lexicon Politi [Calling for Protest: A Political Glossary]*, Tel Aviv: Hakibutz Hameuhad, 2013 [Hebrew].

Hever, Hannan, *With the power of God: Theology and Politics in Modern Hebrew Literature*, Bnei Brak: Hakibutz Hameuhad, 2013 [in Hebrew].

Kristeva, Julia, *Powers of Horror: An Essay on Abjection*, transl. L. S. Roudiez, New York: Columbia University Press, 1982.

Lacan, Jacques, "Kant avec Sade", in *Écrits*, Paris: Seuil, 1966.

Lacan, Jacques, *The Seminar of Jacques Lacan, Book II: The Ego in Freud's Theory and in the Technique of Psychoanalysis*, transl. S. Tomaselli, New York: W.W. Norton, 1991a.

Lacan, Jacques, *The Seminar of Jacques Lacan, Book 1: Freud's Papers on Technique*, 1953–1954, ed. J.-A. Miller, transl. J. Forrester, New York: W.W. Norton & Company, 1991b.

Lacan, Jacques, *The Seminar, Book VII - The Ethics of Psychoanalysis, 1959–1960*, ed. J.-A. Miller, transl. D. Porter, New York: W.W. Norton & Co., 1992.

Lacan, Jacques, *The Seminar, Book III - The Psychoses*, ed. J.-A. Miller, transl. R. Grigg, New York: W.W. Norton & Co., 1993.

Lacan, Jacques, *The Seminar of Jacques Lacan, Book XI: The Four Fundamental Concepts of Psychoanalysis*, transl. A. Sheridan, New York: W.W. Norton, 1998.

Lacan, Jacques, *Écrits*, transl. B. Fink, NY and London: W.W Norton, 2006.

Lacan, Jacques, *The Seminar of Jacques Lacan, Book X: Anxiety*, ed. J.-A. Miller, Cambridge, UK: Polity Books, 2014.

Mouffe, Chantal, *On the Political*, New York: Routledge, 2005.

Nancy, Jean-Luc, *Chroniques Philosophiques*, Paris: Éditions Galilée, 2004.

Ofir, Adi, "Between the Sanctification of Life and Its Abandonment: In Place of an Introduction to Homo Sacer", in *Technologies of Justice: Law, Science, and Society* [in Hebrew], ed. S. Lavi, Tel Aviv: Ramot Publishing, 2003, pp. 353–394.

Ram, Uri and Dani Filc, "The 14th of July of Dafni Leef: The Rise and Fall of the Social Protest", in *Forum: The Social Protest*, ed. U. Ram and D. Filc, *Theory and Criticism 41*, 2013, pp. 17–44 [in Hebrew].

Rousseau, Jean-Jacques, *The Social Contract*, transl. M. Cranston, London: Penguin Books, 1968.

Santner, Eric L., *On the Psychotheology of Everyday Life: Reflections on Freud and Rosenzweig*, Chicago: Chicago University Press, 2001.

Schmitt, Carl, *The Concept of the Political*, transl. G. D. Schwab, Chicago: University of Chicago Press, 1996.

Scholem, Gershom, "Hatzharat Emunim Lasafa Shelanu" ("Declaration of Faith to our Language"), in *Od Davar*, ed. A. Shapira, Tel Aviv: Am Oved, 1989 [in Hebrew].

Weber, Max, *The Protestant Ethic and the Spirit of Capitalism*, transl. T. Parsons, Los Angeles: Roxbury Publishing Company, 1998.

Žižek, Slavoj, *The Puppet and the Dwarf: The Perverse Core of Christianity*, Cambridge, MA: MIT Press, 2003.

Žižek, Slavoj, "Neighbors and Other Monsters: A Plea for Ethical Violence," in *The Neighbor: Three Inquiries in Political Theology*, ed. S. Žižek, E. L. Santner and K. Reinhard, Chicago: University of Chicago Press, 2006.

Index

For Product Safety Concerns and Information please contact our EU
representative GPSR@taylorandfrancis.com
Taylor & Francis Verlag GmbH, Kaufingerstraße 24, 80331 München, Germany

www.ingramcontent.com/pod-product-compliance
Lightning Source LLC
Chambersburg PA
CBHW052012270326
41929CB00015B/2887